BUILDING WEALTH 101

ROBERT BARBERA

THE
MENTORIS
PROJECT

The author has made every effort to ensure the accuracy of the information within this book was correct at time of publication. The author does not assume and hereby disclaims any liability to any party for any loss, damage, or disruption caused by errors or omissions, whether such errors or omissions result from accident, negligence, or any other cause.

Barbera Foundation, Inc.
P.O. Box 1019
Temple City, CA 91780

Copyright © 2021 Barbera Foundation, Inc.
Cover design: Suzanne Turpin

More information at www.mentorisproject.org

ISBN: 978-1-947431-33-1

Library of Congress Control Number: 2021900035

All rights reserved, which includes the right to reproduce this book or portions thereof in any form whatsoever except as provided by the U.S. Copyright Law. For information address Barbera Foundation, Inc.

All net proceeds from the sale of this book will be donated to Barbera Foundation, Inc. whose mission is to support educational initiatives that foster an appreciation of history and culture to encourage and inspire young people to create a stronger future.

Contents

Preface	1
Chapter One: What Is Wealth?	3
Having the Right Mind-Set	4
What They Should Teach You in School (But Don't)	9
Chapter Two: Learning to Budget	15
It's a Good Life	15
Creating Your Own Safety Net	17
Good Life, Good Health Budget	19
Financial Budget	20
Chapter Three: Where Does Your Money Go?	23
Credit Cards	23
Finance Companies and Emergency Loans	27
Premium Spending	27
Discounts	29
Impulse Spending	30
Chapter Four: Smart Spenders and Savers	33
Quality	33
Price	34
Need	35
Free Fun	36
Saving Money	38
Chapter Five: Investing in Yourself	39
Hard Work	42
Supplemental Income	42
Jealousy	44
Naysayers	45
Value	45
Chapter Six: Owning Your Own Home	47
Home Loans	49
Negotiating	49
Investment	52
Leverage	53

Insurance for Your Home	57
Home Equity Loan	58
Home Equity Conversion Mortgage or Reverse Mortgage	59
Disclaimer	59
Chapter Seven: Long-Term Business Growth	**61**
Focus, Not Luck	61
Success and Common Goals	62
Franchise	63
Product	64
Dealership	64
Broker	65
Real Estate Property Management	65
Publishing	67
Mortgages	68
How to Start Your Own Business	69
Niche	70
Business Development	71
Be Relevant	72
Cost Benefit	72
Losing Ideas	73
The Moving Business	73
Housekeeping Service	74
Six Degrees of Connectivity	74
Think Like an Executive	75
Chapter Eight: How Money Works	**77**
Supply and Demand	77
Devaluation of Purchasing Power	78
Inflation	79
Interest	81
Simple vs. Compound Interest	81
Rule of 72	82
Cycles	83
Investment Movement	84
Price Earning Ratio	85

Chapter Nine: Smart Investing	89
Dollar Cost Averaging	89
Investing for Retirement	90
Roth IRA	91
Traditional IRA	92
Roth vs. Traditional IRA	92
Employer-Sponsored Plans	97
College Savings Plan	99
Chapter Ten: Investment Choices	105
Investing in the Stock Market	105
Handling a Windfall	106
What Is the Dow Jones 30 Industrial Average?	107
Standard and Poor's 500	107
What's Going on Behind the Scenes?	108
Stocks	110
Choosing a Broker	114
Bonds	115
Discount Brokers	117
Chapter Eleven: Picking Stocks	119
Evaluating Stocks	120
Things to Avoid in a Stock	121
Things You Want in a Stock	126
Minimizing Risk	128
Don't Quit at the Bottom	129
Having Someone Else Manage Your Money	130
Mutual Funds	132
Exchange Traded Funds	132
The Benefits of Being Cautious	133
Chapter Twelve: Death and Taxes	137
Life Insurance	137
Other Insurance	141
Captive Insurance	142
Annuity	143
Taxes	144

Chapter Thirteen: Your Legacy	149
Retirement	149
Refiring, Not Retiring	150
Foundations	150
Wealth Management	151
Mission	153
About the Author	155
Acknowledgments	156

Preface

This book is meant to help you build a good life. I don't just mean financially, but with health and happiness as well, a life that is worth living. And while that doesn't always take a lot of money, knowing you are on the right path financially can help you to relax and enjoy the journey.

Your life is made up of choices, and the best of those choices provide further opportunities and enable you to strategize for success. You are never too young to start planning. In fact, starting early improves the chances of accomplishing your goal. There are a lot of people who plan only as far as the next vacation, or worse, the next rent payment. That kind of short-term thinking will undercut your chances of long-term success. I don't just want you to plan for your next major life event (marriage/home/family). I want you to plan for events twenty, thirty, even fifty years down the road. Small changes now can reap enormous benefits later.

Time really is money.

But as I said, it's not all about money. Your program should include steps that build a productive and healthy life. That takes initiative on your part. You can't run with the crowd, following the latest craze and diversion. Happiness has to come from you, from actively working to realize the vision you have for yourself. The key to happiness is living for a purpose.

You don't have to take my word for it. Books abound explaining the link between happiness and purpose, the good life and the productive one. I just want to make sure you and I are on the same page, so to speak, and so this is my disclaimer: You are in charge of your choices. You will take my advice or not. You will map this material onto your own life as you see fit. Results may vary because you will vary over the course of your life. As time and circumstances change, it's important to face those new realities and analyze the situation to fit the future you want to live into.

Whoever you are and wherever you may be on your life's journey, there is something in this book for you. The interesting thing is it may not be what you expect. You may be in your twenties and think there's nothing in the section on "Refiring" that has any connection to your life right now. But I'm going to bet if you take a look, you'll find something about your purpose, your legacy, and other avenues you might want to pursue that could have an impact on how you live your life today. By the same token, there's sure to be something about developing the right mind-set that someone in their fifties may think is directed only at young people—but let me tell you, it's never too late to get yourself on the path to success. My hope is that you'll read the book cover to cover and then come back often to dip into the chapters that you need most at different points in your life.

I wish you luck. More, I wish you an amazing future.

Let's get started.

Chapter One

What Is Wealth?

This book was designed to provide fundamental concepts, and the most fundamental concept of all is: What do we mean by the term *wealth*?

You may think you know—and you're partially right. You know exactly what wealth means to you today, at nineteen or twenty-two or twenty-eight. Maybe it means summers in exotic locations, or maybe it means having enough to not have to worry about rent, or maybe it means treating your friends to pizza. But I'm going to bet you've never sat down and figured out exactly what it could mean over the course of your lifetime. It's a pretty safe bet, because most people never sit down to think about what wealth really means.

Wealth is not just money. It is the capacity to enjoy what we have without constantly grasping for more. There is a freedom to wealth, but it's more than just the freedom of not needing to worry about how you'll pay for the basics. It's the freedom of living your life to the fullest.

For me, a key strategy that gave me the feeling of wealth even when my wife and I were living paycheck to paycheck was knowing we had a *plan*.

Let me backtrack a little. I want to provide you with a systematic understanding of the many possibilities for creating income so you can see the raw material you have to plan with. There are a lot of paths to wealth, which is a good thing because not everyone will have the same opportunities. But one opportunity that is equally open to every one of us is deciding that we want to place a value on our future.

There is a saying that the world is your oyster. Unfortunately, too many people close their futures off and keep that oyster tightly shut by living for today rather than investing in tomorrow. If you want to live into a terrific future, you have to choose it. You have to plan for it. Choices and opportunities will change over time, but if you are mindful of the future, you can take advantage of whatever is available to you now. The other thing a plan provides is positive reinforcement. It will amaze you to watch your plan unfold, to reach your benchmarks. It will help you to enjoy the journey as well as the destination.

Aim high. Choose an arena you genuinely enjoy. I love real estate; I've loved it my whole life. When I was a kid, I read contracts to my mother, whose English wasn't quite up to the legal jargon, but whose brain could always see the possibilities and the pitfalls. You never wanted to be up against her in a negotiation. I loved managing apartment buildings, I loved fixing them up and keeping tenants happy, and I really loved the art of the deal when it came to financing the buildings. While I've done a lot of things that have worked out for me financially, I've only ever done things I was truly able to enjoy. It's been a lot of fun.

But that's me. I know people who would prefer to do anything else with their life rather than be a landlord. They have other skills they'd rather use to build their financial future. They became lawyers, doctors, writers, artists, entrepreneurs . . . although these days, *everyone* is an entrepreneur. The time of putting your financial well-being into the hands of a single employer from high school to retirement is long gone.

This is the first mind-set shift you need to make: You are one hundred percent responsible for your career and your financial future. You are both the CEO and CFO of You, Inc.

Having the Right Mind-Set

There is an old phrase that I learned as an accounting major:

"Gobbledygook going in will result in gobbledygook coming out." What the accountant is saying is that if information is poorly entered into the books, then the records will come out incorrect. I understand that computer coders have co-opted it in recent years, but the sentiment predated programming. In fact, human beings have been grappling with this idea for centuries: You are who you are because of the choices you make.

The more you grow as an individual and the better the decisions you make, the more you will build not only your future, but also your character. Start by assessing where you are right now, today. Do you want to be in a production industry? A service industry? What are your talents? What kind of people do you want to spend your days with?

Now, who do you want to be?

Without doubt, you have a lot of terrific traits. You're smart, you're inquisitive, you're resilient, you're loyal, you're thoughtful . . . I could go on and on. You are many wonderful things. Go ahead, write them all down.

Equally without doubt, you have some issues. I can say this with complete confidence because you are human. You might procrastinate or give up on yourself or others, or walk into a room with anger rather than curiosity. But the more you utilize your positive strengths, the more opportunities you will be able to take advantage of.

Really think about who you want to be in the world. Is there someone you admire? Someone successful whose path you might want to emulate? I don't want you to think about them in terms of the opportunities they had, because your life is different; even the world is different now from when they started out. Rather, I want you to think about their attitude. How do they approach business? Life? Other people? Adversity?

How do you approach these things?

Take a minute to see yourself as other people see you. Where can you adjust your attitude to match the kind of person you wish to be? For instance, let's take how you approach a setback. If you see it as unfair or as a personal attack, or as the forever end of all your hopes and dreams, you will shut down. That setback will cost you so much more because you won't be able to bounce back. But if, instead, you decide to see each setback as temporary, as an opportunity for you to be creative about getting around it, or as a chance to learn and grow, you'll be open to feedback that can only improve your chances of success next time. You will see secondary opportunities that you had missed the first time around. Most of all, by behaving with dignity and determination, you'll maintain relationships that can help you in the future. Be someone other people want to work with, someone other people want to help, because they see you as someone who will be able to help them in return down the road. You can build your network through adversity as well as through success, but only if your attitude is professional, competent, and respectful.

You also need to have a plan. Where do you want to be in the future? Have your destiny fixed in your own mind's eye and see it clearly. See yourself succeeding beyond your wildest dreams. What does it look like to have all your goals fulfilled? How will you feel? Think about the many challenges you had to overcome to reach your goal. Feel proud of yourself for having overcome all of them.

Now look back to today. You have a goal firmly in place and you can still picture how amazing it will feel when you have achieved it. How are you going to get there? What's your first milestone? What are the challenges that are either already upon you or might come up in the future? Really think about the obstacles you might face. Don't let them deter you; rather, come up with a plan for how you will overcome those challenges.

For instance, a lot of financial advice centers on having savings to cover six months of unemployment. That may seem an impossible goal, or it may seem to be a safety net you'll never need. But the benefit of having money socked away isn't just that you may find yourself unemployed. Knowing you have that safety net can free you to make better decisions. You don't have to stay stuck in a terrible job or an unsafe living situation if you have enough savings to smooth over a temporary change. Knowing you have a choice allows you to make a *good* choice, a choice to invest in yourself and your future. In the same way, planning for challenges and obstacles, and putting safety nets in place to offset those possible problems, will free you up to see opportunities and make good choices because you're not living in fear. You have a plan.

One important safety net is your network. Your relationships will help you find and succeed at jobs and will be there for you as references, sounding boards, and resources. There's some validity to the idea that you are the sum of the six people you spend the most time with. I'm not saying you should ditch your friends, but I am saying be aware of spending time with people who support your goals. You will all rise together, helping each other, working together, introducing each other to yet more people who will support your future. Make sure you are always developing new relationships with people in your field (or the field you want to be in), and ideally develop relationships with people a little further along on the journey than you are (more on how to do that later). What you will learn from them informally is priceless.

You also need to be the kind of person they want to hang around. Make sure your friends and associates respect you as a person. Be someone they can respect, and surround yourself with people you genuinely respect. Contempt is a relationship killer.

Another part of the plan needs to be your education. I'm not just talking about high school and college, although today it's hard to break in anywhere without a degree. Here are some different ways you need to be on top of things:

- Educate yourself about your field. What are the trade journals, what websites do people in the field read, where do they get their information on the state and future of their profession? Read those.

- What are the professional organizations that people join? Where are there in-person meetings or online groups? Can you join as an aspiring or new member of the profession?

- What skills do you need to succeed? Where can you learn those skills, either online or perhaps at a local community college? In person is always better because you will meet a professor and other students in your industry. This is a great way to expand your network.

- Keep an open mind and be on the lookout for anyone who can help you better yourself in your field. Be willing to do the grunt work necessary to prove yourself and learn how the business actually functions. Sometimes, taking a job as an assistant is as good as getting a graduate degree—even better, if you're the one making appointments and taking notes in meetings. You will get to know all the players personally, as well as seeing firsthand how decisions get made.

Don't be afraid to be a beginner. You don't have to know it all; listen to other people's views and advice. Be patient. To be a leader, you need to follow first.

You also need to be willing to buck convention. Without being foolish, take the time to look at the other side of things; when the whole world is reacting one way, consider the opposite. The great example of this is the stock market. When everyone else is going crazy and selling off their stocks, if you can keep your head and instead buy when stocks are low, you will make a fortune in the long run. Advancement comes by breaking through the status quo, thinking of new ways to tackle old problems. Our great thinkers and inventors continually broke the mold. How crazy was Leonardo da Vinci? He designed a helicopter during the Renaissance! How crazy were the Wright Brothers to think they could do what no human being had ever done (other than Icarus, and we know how that turned out) and fly? And yet few are more revered for creativity than Leonardo, or for the results of their invention than Wilbur and Orville Wright. Be inventive in every part of your life, your career, and your business. It's not just a key to success—it's also a lot of fun.

Your culture also has an impact on your core values and even what you believe is possible. The United States of America has developed its own code, including a rugged individuality straight out of the Wild West, but coupled with a core value of morality and fairness. We strive not to leave anyone behind. We also believe in level playing fields and opportunity in abundance for any individual to pursue the life they want.

Life is change; what's important is to face those changes from a foundation of values that you subscribe to and truly embrace. Everything will continue to change: technology, our political system, the economy, even our social structure. So much has changed in my lifetime alone. The key for you is to cope by reacting to change head-on. Understand your values and move forward with focus and a belief that change represents opportunity. If you are honorable and working toward the good of your family, your neighbors, and your country, then what you are doing will help make the changes good for everyone.

What They Should Teach You in School (But Don't)

Unfortunately, as society and our daily lives have changed, our educational system has not kept up the pace. For the most part, you learned the same things I learned when I went to high school—and it's going to be about as useful to you, which is not saying much. Even college may not offer much in the way of practical education. Without completely dismissing the importance of knowing how to read, write, and count, I must point out that there are so many other critical life skills completely ignored by schools. Chief among them is financial planning.

There are basic budgeting practices that are the foundation for building a solid future. You need to know how to write a check. And while online banking gives you a daily snapshot of your bank accounts, you still need to make sure that more goes in each month than needs to come out. Math is a particularly useful skill when you're totaling up your obligations—rent, utility, student loans—and matching them against your income. Let's hope you never need that lesson on negative numbers.

Since school is not likely to prepare you for life, you're going to need to learn financial skills on your own. Upcoming chapters will include budgeting, credit cards, home loans, and saving for retirement, among a lot of other things. But turn on your antenna now and be on the lookout for anything that can help you gain foundational financial skills. Read the finance section of your local newspaper. Listen to a podcast on financial well-being. Talk to people who have made money in different ways and ask them about their financial strategies—and about their mistakes. That kind of learning is priceless.

Schools should also do a better job of preparing students for a career. I don't just mean in terms of hard skills, but also career planning. I have given presentations at several high schools and met hundreds of high school seniors. I talked to them about making career choices, and it broke my heart to see that they were not prepared. Many had no concept at all of how to make career choices. It killed me to watch young adults move into dead-end positions. I was driven to try to find a way to help.

I made it my job to contribute in a practical way whenever possible. I went to JCPenney and bought kids the right clothes for an interview. I gave them training in how to apply for a job and interview well; I even set up some interviews for them. But one of the most important things I did was to develop a questionnaire to help them see what choices they had and where their aptitude might best fit. I'll talk more about that in a minute.

Now, ideally, this kind of thing is done in high school, with your college counselor, or in college with a career advisor. The fact that I was the one doing it spoke to how overwhelmed our schools are and how ill-equipped they are to help the hundreds of thousands of students who go through their doors every year. But one of the many things I've learned in life is that you should always be on the lookout for good information and how you can learn from others. Seek out people who can help you clarify your vision for your future, both in school and in the world. Is there someone whose job sounds interesting to you? Ask them to talk about it with you. How did they get into it? What skills did they need to learn? What do they enjoy about it? People love to talk about themselves! Let them give you a glimpse at a possible career for yourself.

Back to the questionnaire. I didn't do a formal, bubble-in-the-answer questionnaire; what I did was sit and ask questions and listen.

I can't do that for you right now, but I can let you in on the kinds of questions you should be asking yourself—and you don't have to be a high school senior to take it, either. Start wherever you are.

- Take stock right now. How old are you? Are you employed (full-time or part-time)? What do you like about your job? What about friends and siblings? Who has a job, what kind of job is it, and do they enjoy it?

- Let's look at where you came from. Growing up, what did your parents do? What about your aunts/uncles/neighbors? Don't underestimate how important it is to know people who do different jobs. There's a reason children go into the family business: It's what they know. But it may not be the right business for you. The more contact you've had with people in different professions, the more your imagination can offer you different possibilities for your future.

- What standard of life do you want to have? Be specific. "Rich" means different things to different people. Think about it in terms of doing work you love and not having to worry about money. What would that look like? How much would you have to bring in every month for that lifestyle to be possible for you?

- What career do you envision for yourself? If you're not sure, what work do you see yourself doing and enjoying? How can you contribute to the world? Do you know anyone who works in that field? Who can you reach out to and ask about their career paths?

- What skills do you have? What skills do you need? Education—and I'm talking about knowledge that is beyond what you learn in high school and college—is the game-changer, and there are so many ways today to learn things, both online and in person. Make a list of skills you need and find someone who can teach you, either in a school or online setting, or by watching someone who already has that skill. Don't discount "soft" skills; coding is good in today's world, but people skills are just as valuable.

One more time, let me underscore the value of an education. No matter what field you're interested in, someone is out there teaching people how to get better at it. If you don't commit to lifelong education and start today, you are forever curtailing your chances. Ambition is good, dreams are great, but you have to be willing to put in the work, and at its most basic level, that means learning the ropes.

I also talked with students about grooming and interview attitude. The short version is this: You want to look like someone who already has the job. They need to be able to envision you in that position. Get a haircut. Look professional. Be polite. Know what you would be able to contribute to their organization. No one is going to give you a job because you need one; they're going to give you a job because they need you.

Why am I focusing on this? Shouldn't this book be all about the secret sauce to becoming wealthy? Here's what other books won't tell you: The actual secret sauce isn't a secret at all. *Have more money coming in than going out.* That's it. When you have more money coming in, you can try new things, invest in yourself, make mistakes, and leverage small amounts to create large amounts.

The problem isn't that there's a secret to building wealth; the problem is that the real path isn't glamorous! It's not betting on the stock market or turning around a failing business. Although both of those things can lead to wealth, they're an end game, after years of experience, failure, and learning by doing. They are not shortcuts. No, the real secret is having the ability to move up in your career and the freedom to choose an even better career when you find one. That takes a level of security that comes from having more income than outgo, month after month.

Don't go into a dead-end job. If you need the money, take a job on weekends or at night, but do not get sucked into a full-time job that pays just enough to live on with no real opportunity for advancement. Spend your days in a job that offers you a future, or in getting the training you need to get to that next step on the ladder.

I realize this is a complicated choice. Sometimes, the need for a job seems overwhelming and you will take the first thing you can get. If that has happened to you, don't despair. You can build your way even out of a dead-end job. You have two options: Spend less or earn more. Either way, you can build a financial cushion that will allow you to take steps to improve your situation. Budgeting and second jobs (or side hustles) are both covered later in the book. When you do both of these things together, you can transform your life.

Finally, getting a job is about more than just having money to spend. Yes, it's very important that you have a reliable income, and a steady paycheck can also help you create savings that will in turn help you leverage your resources toward building greater wealth (more on this later). But having a job is also critical because it reminds you that you are employable—that you can always get another job, a better job, a more interesting job. I've quit several jobs in my life, and I always left without the slightest worry of finding another because I knew I had skills and relationships and I could always land another job. Talk about freedom! Knowing you will always land on your feet gives you the freedom to improve your situation. Even if you decide to stay in a less-than-perfect job, the decision comes from a place of strength, which means you'll do a better job, make better contacts, impress those who are higher up the ladder, and continue to grow in a way you wouldn't if you felt imprisoned by your day job. We've all met people who hate what they do and yet don't make a change. It's not the kind of life you ever have to live. Because you hold the keys to your own future, you can always make a better choice.

This is one of the ways in which this book is for more than just those who are starting out in life (although I see you, and I believe this book will help set you on the right track). Many of the things I talk about are applicable at almost any point in your life. In fact, I talk about refiring your work when you hit midlife and become bored with your career; I cover investing in the stock market, which is a smart move no matter what your age; and I discuss what makes life worth living and how you want to be remembered. No matter if you're eighteen or eighty-one, this book offers counsel as you reshape your destiny and redirect your energies. Life is full of surprises, including many new opportunities for you to develop, if only you keep a lookout for them.

Chapter Two

Learning to Budget

Let me start by saying that everyone has their own comfort level, their own baseline for how they want to live day to day. We are influenced by so many things—where we live, how we grew up, what our friends and neighbors and siblings have, and even what we see in magazines, on TV, and on the internet. But here's the thing: The way we choose to live today has a lasting impact on our future. It's not that I don't want you to have a nice car or expensive shoes. I just don't want you to trade your future security for it.

It's a Good Life

It used to be that we had little to no choice in our career path. For most of history, we lived a life we were born into. We worked the farm, followed in the family business, or married the boy next door. Our destiny was to a large extent determined by the circumstances of our birth. Today, we can influence our future to an extent that even our great-grandparents would have found astonishing. But with that freedom comes responsibility: the responsibility of making good choices.

The key word here is *choice*. Good choices will keep you from falling into the abyss of living paycheck to paycheck. Many times, I have seen people earning the same salary that I did, but living totally different lifestyles with bigger houses, newer cars, and higher levels of debt. And let me tell you, with debt comes regret.

In fact, there are two different kinds of debt: good debt, when you're leveraging other people's money to create value and wealth; and bad debt, when you trade tomorrow's security on something you want today.

Good debt is something we're going to talk a lot about later. Right now, I'm interested in bad debt, and in helping you avoid it.

You can't live the Good Life if bad habits take control. What do I mean by the Good Life? It's when you prosper financially and you have something to show for it. It's the security of knowing that even if something terrible happens, you won't end up on the street. I mean this quite literally. We stretched ourselves financially, my first wife and I, in order to buy a multi-unit apartment building, but if something had gone wrong—if we weren't able to fill enough units to meet our debt payments, for example—we always could have sold our house and lived in the building ourselves. It wouldn't have been ideal, but it also wouldn't have been terrible. We wouldn't have gone bankrupt, we wouldn't have lost everything, we wouldn't have ended up on the street. We had young children, so no matter what our ambitions, we couldn't risk their well-being. For us, real estate provided a path to wealth while at the same time giving us a built-in safety net if things went wrong. The freedom to go big comes from being creative and figuring out a way to risk a lot without risking it all.

You also need to be creative in how you solve problems. For instance, at one point, I had two problems. First, I had an apartment building with eighty-eight residential units and five shops on the ground floor. One of those shops, I just couldn't rent; it was empty and it stayed empty, and that wasn't good for the location or for my bottom line. My second problem was that I had a terrific manager, one I wanted to keep, only her boyfriend was out of work. And then a third problem popped up, one that had an impact on how easy or difficult it would be to rent my apartments: The local grocery store closed. So here's what I did. I bought the guy's grocery store, all his fixtures and remaining inventory, and moved it into my empty storefront unit. And I hired my manager's boyfriend to run the place. He didn't have any experience in retail, and obviously the grocer himself hadn't been able to make enough money to keep going, so how would we do better? By being smarter.

I realized that people came home hungry; they wanted prepared food that was easy to grab and go. So we added simple stuff—hot dogs, barbecue, rotisserie. It took an investment of a little more equipment, but everyone ended up happy: my tenants, my manager, and my bottom line, as rent was now being paid from the grocery store's operating budget. Did I make money on the grocery itself? No! I took a loss there, but I kept my wonderful manager, my tenants were happy to have a grocery store so close, and I got rental income out of it. It was a creative solution and part of a bigger picture. Always look to see how you can make the best with whatever you have going.

Creating Your Own Safety Net

Think about what it will take for you to create your own financial safety net.

Step one: What is the bare minimum you could live on and be okay? Not go hungry, not live in your car, not put at risk anyone who depends on you?

Step two: Now that you have that figure, how can you build in a safety net so that your minimum requirement is never in danger?

There are a couple of ways to do this. The first is to build an emergency fund. Everyone suggests that you do this, and for good reason. This is cash you can tap into when things go south—and they will. In everyone's life, things go wrong. When I was young and dabbling in the stock market, I had my entire investment wiped out one day. That was a hard lesson, but it was a lesson, not a disaster, because I hadn't invested more than I could lose and still survive. (Let me give another plug here for the day job, which meant I still had money coming in.)

The other reason to work on building an emergency fund is so you'll start developing the habit of saving. Putting your money away not just to prevent disaster, but also to build a fund that will allow you to start investing in your future—that's priceless. But it takes dedication, and you can begin to develop that muscle today by setting money aside in a rainy day fund. Start small, but start.

How can you start today? You could get a jar and stick five dollars in it. I'm not kidding. Go without a latte, take the bus to work instead of gassing up the car, do whatever you need to do so you won't spend that five dollars today. (And don't just put it on your credit card. I'll talk a lot more about credit cards later, but for now, let's just call it cheating.) But better than money in a jar is money in the bank. It requires thinking to put money in a jar—and willpower not to take it out—but setting up an automatic transfer from your checking account to your savings account is a no-brainer. Set it up to put aside money every time your paycheck gets deposited so you never see that part of your paycheck. It trains you to live on less than you make, which is an important first step, and it builds that all-important savings account passively. A bonus, birthday money, a windfall—all of those should go into your savings account, not your checking account. You're not buying the latest electronic gadget with it, but you are buying your future.

Another way to build your safety net so your minimum requirement is never in danger is to develop good spending habits. Bad spending habits will undercut you at every turn. If you borrow today, assuming you can pay it back when you get that bonus or that pay raise or commission, I guarantee that not only will you overspend now, but you will also find that the bonus/raise/commission will only cause you to spend even more. Either your baseline outgo is below your income and you're fine, or it's above your income and you are in serious trouble. Train yourself now to spend less and you will be rewarded throughout your life.

Because here's the thing about the Good Life: It's not about what toys you have. It's about financial prosperity, feeling secure about the future, knowing you can take care of yourself and the people who count on you. There are lots of fun things you can do for free—going for walks, hanging out with friends (potlucks, not restaurants!), reading books and watching movies that you borrow from the library, not to mention taking advantage of free community events like concerts and parades. The truth is, living the Good Life isn't nearly as dependent on how much comes in as it is on how much goes out.

Good Life, Good Health Budget

The other part of the Good Life is to have good health and stay energized. Your effectiveness for everything depends on your health. Taking care of yourself means that you can take care of others—and take care of business.

When you're young, you think you are indestructible. In fact, studies suggest that your brain doesn't even learn to assess risk properly until you're in your mid-twenties. So I guess it's natural that you think you can eat, drink, do drugs, and carry on with destructive behavior because it seems to you that your young body tolerates bad choices. But it's really not that your body is able to tolerate abuse. Rather, just like a credit card, your body is keeping track of bad health choices, storing them up and presenting you with a staggering total later in life.

People knew smoking was bad for you even when I was a young boy. I remember we were told not to smoke, that the consequences would include shortness of breath and that our growth would be stunted. Nevertheless, both my brother and my dad ignored this advice and just smoked away. Later in life, they could not break their smoking habit. Both died of smoking-related issues. So I won't lie—this one is personal to me. New ways of smoking such as vaping and e-cigarettes have also shown harmful long-term effects. Do yourself a favor and don't start; if you have started, do everything you can to quit now. Don't subject your body to toxic smoke and your family to both secondhand smoke and the pain that comes with losing you to a preventable illness.

Drugs, even when prescribed, can lead to a dangerous outcome. Every few years one drug or another is shown to have resulted in unintended consequences, and I'm sure I don't have to tell you the toll opioids have taken in the last decade. And these are the legal drugs! You must be careful in the use of any drug. Safeguard your own health; we've learned the hard way that even doctors won't safeguard it for you.

Really, the key to all of this is that everything should be taken in moderation. It used to be that we worked hard on the farm and got plenty of exercise just getting food on the table—and that food was mostly fresh, not full of salt or fat or all the chemicals they throw in it today. Replicate that if you can. Don't fall into the trap of thinking that being wealthy means eating rich food and lounging around all day, every day. That leads to obesity and diabetes, not health, wealth, and happiness.

Create good habits with your health just as you create good habits with your money. You need both. Not to mention the fact that a lot of health killers (cigarettes, drugs, too much alcohol or rich foods) are expensive. You already know what you should be doing, and I'm not a doctor, so I'm not going to give you that kind of advice. Here is the advice I will give you: Don't throw money at getting and staying healthy. In fact, make it a game.

Where your health "budget" and your financial budget interact is when improving your health either helps you save money or costs you money. See how much you can do to improve your health without spending a dime. Go for morning walks, meditate on a cushion from your couch, do push-ups, dance around your house. I know one woman who took charge of her healthy eating by cooking herself a fresh meal every night. She didn't have a lot of money and had to limit her salt intake for medical reasons, so she decided rather than eat out or order in, she would make cooking her hobby. She would find a new recipe, stop at the store on her way home from work, and cook something fun every night. It taught her a skill, gave her something to look forward to, and improved her health at the same time. Make it a game, one that reflects your own personality, and play it to the hilt. You will reap the rewards of good health for the rest of your life.

Okay, let's get down to the nitty-gritty.

Financial Budget

Not having a budget is like traveling without a map. Guessing will not get you to your destination. No matter what size your paycheck may be, you will never be sure where your money is going without a budget.

So let's take a crack at it now. At the end of this chapter is a worksheet for you to plug your numbers into. There may be things here you haven't considered.

The trick here is to make sure that 1) the expenses are equal to or less than the income, and 2) every month, you are putting some money into investments. That's where your future lives.

The point of this exercise is to show you things you probably don't even think about. Home ownership includes homeowner's insurance and property taxes. Transportation is car payments, car insurance, gas, and maintenance. Food is both groceries and eating out. You may find other expenses you have on a regular basis that you need to include; you can finesse the budget over the next few months. And look how I didn't include any money for entertainment! Remember, my default is to go for free entertainment. When I was just getting started, my wife and I watched a lot of television! Not cable, either—just free, over-the-airwaves TV. Cut discretionary income wherever you can. The point is to start somewhere.

Start by keeping track of exactly where your money goes. Look at your bank and credit card statements for any recurring charges. Pull out all your receipts. Don't judge, but do gather data. Get as complete a picture as you can of three to six months' worth of expenses and average out from there. Yes, this will take some time, but consider it an investment in your future. You can't move forward if you don't have a grip on where your money goes, and most people are surprised to find out what is really happening with their money.

Remember that any budget can be adjusted over time. As you read this book, I hope you'll adjust some of your expenses as well as your income. You can prepare a fresh budget as both your situation and your goals shift. Later we will talk about your investment account, that next step beyond the "rainy day" savings account. The old adage "It's not what you make, but what you keep" is so true.

I love budgeting. Remember how I suggested you make staying on a budget a game? Keeping a budget is like a scorecard, and these stats keep you in control. At first it's bothersome, but as the habit sets in, it becomes second nature. The result of actually looking at where you put your money and deliberately living within a budget will change your perspective on what is worthless and what is really valuable.

ROBERT BARBERA

BUDGET WORKSHEET

	YEARLY TOTAL
INCOME	
MAIN JOB	
SIDE HUSTLE	
TOTAL INCOME	
LESS INCOME TAXES	
NET INCOME	
EXPENSES	
LIVING EXPENSES	
RENT/MORTGAGE	
PROPERTY TAXES	
TRANSPORTATION	
CAR INSURANCE	
RENTERS/HOMEOWNERS INSURANCE	
MEDICAL INSURANCE	
UTILITIES	
FOOD	
CLOTHING	
REPAYMENT OF COLLEGE LOANS	
TOTAL LIVING EXPENSES	
INVESTMENTS	
EMERGENCY SAVINGS	
LIFE INSURANCE	
CHILDREN'S COLLEGE TUITION	
IRA	
MISCELLANEOUS	
TOTAL INVESTMENTS	

(TOTAL LIVING EXPENSES) + (TOTAL INVESTMENTS) = TOTAL EXPENSES

NET INCOME MINUS TOTAL EXPENSES SHOULD EQUAL ZERO

Chapter Three

Where Does Your Money Go?

Budgeting helps us keep track of where our money goes, but there are some sneaky ways it can slip through our fingers. Let's look at a few of the common pitfalls along with some ideas to cut back on spending.

Credit Cards

Credit cards can be extremely useful because they are easier than cash, especially for large purchases, but they can also be extremely destructive to your financial health for exactly the same reason. A credit card facilitates our money transactions in several ways:

- We don't have to carry around cash or write checks.

- We can get advances on our money needs.

- It enables us to feel like we can spend more than we otherwise would.

- It often provides earning incentives, e.g., travel rewards or gift cards to stores.

Now before you start thinking that I'm anti-credit card, you should know that I'm really not. Credit cards can be used to your advantage, whether they give you cash back or you use the credit line they offer to make a critical purchase for your business. But they should always be used with caution.

Credit card companies are in business to make money. They often promote their card to you even if you already have more credit than you can afford. People spend time hunting for coupons and discount codes, but they don't bother to pay off their credit cards every month, which results in interest fees and penalties that vastly increase the cost of the thing they bought "on sale."

If you don't think the interest rate is a significant amount, take a look at the table on the next two pages. It shows how someone with a credit card with a balance of $9,000 ends up paying about $5,000 **in interest alone** in just under four years. This is based on making a $300 monthly payment with an interest rate of 25 percent, and *not putting another dime on the credit card* in the meantime.

A $9,000 debt becomes nearly a $14,000 one. Everything you bought with this card cost you more than 50 percent above sticker price. Credit cards may be convenient, but they are very expensive if you don't pay off the entire balance every month.

Another common misconception people have is that the more credit cards they own, the higher their credit score will be. But the fact is the more credit you use, the lower your score drops. Each transaction you make using your credit card will decrease your credit score.

Added to this is the very real danger that you will misuse your credit cards. They are designed to encourage you to spend without thinking about whether or not you have the money right now to pay for whatever it is you're buying. One of the reasons credit cards look so good to the consumer is that the more credit you are approved for, the more you believe you can spend. Remember that credit card companies make a lot of money off of people who, in fact, cannot afford to pay off their cards. They often bring you in by offering no interest for

CREDIT CARD DEBT EXAMPLE

[$9,000 BALANCE]

MONTH	PAYMENT	25% INTEREST PAID	BALANCE DUE
OPENING	$0	0	$9,000
JANUARY	$300	$183	$8,883
FEBRUARY	$300	$181	$8,764
MARCH	$300	$179	$8,643
APRIL	$300	$176	$8,519
MAY	$300	$173	$8,392
JUNE	$300	$171	$8,263
JULY	$300	$168	$8,131
AUGUST	$300	$165	$7,997
SEPTEMBER	$300	$163	$7,860
OCTOBER	$300	$160	$7,719
NOVEMBER	$300	$157	$7,576
DECEMBER	$300	$154	$7,430
TOTAL PAID YEAR 1	**$3,600**	**$2,030**	
JANUARY	$300	$151	$7,281
FEBRUARY	$300	$148	$7,129
MARCH	$300	$145	$6,973
APRIL	$300	$141	$6,815
MAY	$300	$138	$6,653
JUNE	$300	$135	$6,488
JULY	$300	$131	$6,319
AUGUST	$300	$128	$6,147
SEPTEMBER	$300	$124	$5,971
OCTOBER	$300	$121	$5,792
NOVEMBER	$300	$117	$5,609
DECEMBER	$300	$113	$5,422
TOTAL PAID YEAR 2	**$3,600**	**$1,592**	

CREDIT CARD DEBT EXAMPLE (CONTINUED)

MONTH	PAYMENT	25% INTEREST PAID	BALANCE DUE
JANUARY	$300	$109	$5,231
FEBRUARY	$300	$105	$5,037
MARCH	$300	$101	$4,838
APRIL	$300	$97	$4,635
MAY	$300	$93	$4,428
JUNE	$300	$89	$4,217
JULY	$300	$84	$4,001
AUGUST	$300	$80	$3,781
SEPTEMBER	$300	$75	$3,556
OCTOBER	$300	$71	$3,327
NOVEMBER	$300	$66	$3,092
DECEMBER	$300	$61	$2,853
TOTAL PAID YEAR 3	**$3,600**	**$1,031**	
JANUARY	$300	$56	$2,609
FEBRUARY	$300	$51	$2,360
MARCH	$300	$46	$2,106
APRIL	$300	$41	$1,847
MAY	$300	$35	$1,582
JUNE	$300	$30	$1,312
JULY	$300	$24	$1,036
AUGUST	$300	$18	$754
SEPTEMBER	$300	$13	$467
OCTOBER	$300	$7	$173
NOVEMBER	$177	$4	$0
TOTAL PAID YEAR 4	**$3,177**	**$325**	

TOTAL INTEREST PAID OVER 4 YEARS: $ 4,978
TOTAL AMOUNT PAID OVER 4 YEARS: $ 13,978

a year, and they use that year to train you to NOT pay off your debt every month, because for those first twelve months, there are no repercussions. Which makes it all the more devastating when the exorbitant interest rate kicks in later. So take any credit offer with a grain of salt. Just because you have the line of credit doesn't mean you can afford to use it.

Because inevitably something does go wrong. That's why we need an emergency fund, and that's why we don't want to back ourselves into a corner and get mired in high-interest credit card debt. Use credit cards sparingly, and if you find you can't pay them off every month, stop using them entirely until that debt is paid. Otherwise, you are destroying your cash flow and pouring money down the drain—money you could be using to build your own wealth.

Finance Companies and Emergency Loans

The worst possible option if you do find yourself in a financial hole is to take out an emergency loan. This would be an extremely costly consequence of not taking control of your finances and not having a backup plan in place. The annual percentage rate of these emergency loans can range from 155 percent to a whopping 460 percent. Here's what that means: Borrowing $2,500 now will cost you at least $5,000 over the course of the next twelve months, and even more if you take longer than a year to pay it back. So whatever it is you think you need to buy for $2,500 will actually cost you at least $5,000. That is the real price tag of the item. You have to ask yourself: Is this something for which you really want to pay double the cost? And, often, are you willing to risk your car as collateral to get it?

Do not get sucked into these loans; they can destroy any chance you have of getting on your feet financially.

Premium Spending

So how do you not get into this mess in the first place?

Spend less money than you have coming in.

That's it. That is the one thing you absolutely have to understand. There is no magic involved. You need to have more money coming in every month than you have going out.

There are two ways to do this and I recommend both:

- Spend less.

- Make more.

Much of this book is devoted to making more, but for now I want to talk about spending less. Buy less and spend less on what you do buy. Premium products may be of better quality. But they may also simply be new or trendy. Often new products test the price for early buyers, people who love being first. If you don't need the bragging rights (and here's a hint—you *never* need the bragging rights), wait a while and you will see a price reduction.

Many people will advise you to spend on quality because it lasts longer. Sometimes this is true. But it's not always true enough to make a difference. When paying a premium for something, it may have the same functionality as something of lesser cost. For instance, a watch. A gold Rolex watch priced at $6,000 tells the same time as a $100 Timex watch. Is it worth it to pay for the premium brand to achieve the same end of telling time? No. In fact, you actually don't need a watch at all these days because you almost certainly have a phone. Understand a watch for what it really is: a status symbol.

Labels are another way of paying premiums because there is cachet to a "name." All that means is there's a social belief that if a manufacturer puts a label on something, it's worth more. Really. It's all smoke and mirrors.

Do you want to look like you are a successful businessperson or do you want to *actually be* a successful businessperson? A good businessperson knows a good deal when they see one; they also know when they are being hoodwinked. Don't kid yourself that looking the part is half the battle. It isn't. Having the money to invest—in yourself, in your business, in the stock market, in real estate—is the real battle. Don't toss your future away on something designed simply to part you from as much of your money as possible. Marketing is a tool to try to lead you to believe the premium is worth the purchase.

Even events, where you are buying an experience, can be had for less. It's amazing to see the difference in ticket prices at the same event, depending on what location you're sitting in. Front seating may be the most expensive, but the theater design and acoustics may provide the best sound further back. Once the curtain rises, the cheaper seats enjoy the same performance.

Whether it's a watch or a sweater or an experience, you can often buy the same thing without the label and without the premium and have it work just as well. And that extra savings, over time, can make the difference between being able to swing buying your first property, paying off your college loans, or investing in a business—or having to wait another year.

Discounts

Discounting goods is another merchandise incentive. Some people actually believe they're saving money even as they are spending money. What a fantastic act of mesmerizing the public! Sellers will actually get you to think that they are doing you a favor, when, in fact, you are forking over your hard-earned cash to them. What people fail to realize is that the discount price was planned. Companies are still making money on the discounted price once that premium price I mentioned earlier has lured in all the early adopters, the ones who have to have it right away.

Look at movie theater prices. Generally, movies that are opening are not available for discounted tickets on that first weekend. But wait two weeks and you can use that gift certificate your brother gave you. In those two weeks, that movie has not changed one frame. The only thing that's changed is that the people who wanted to be the first to see it have moved on to the next "first." Being willing to see a film that's a few weeks old, or to see something at a time other than a Friday or Saturday night, gives you more choices in terms of price point, but doesn't change the quality of what you're seeing in the least.

The creation of "trends" in fashions, styles, and colors every year is an attempt to convince you that you need to throw away the old and buy the new. As the son of a fashion designer who made his living creating a new season every year, let me tell you: Don't fall for it. Buy something you look good in. Wear it. Shop at consignments or discount stores; wait until the end of the season to buy for next year. If you want to be really frugal, check out thrift stores. Developing your own style means that you are always in fashion.

The axiom is "buyer beware." The art of marketing entices you to buy more. The best time to buy Christmas cards is in January; get them early for next year. By the same token, buy holiday gifts in the slow months or in post-holiday sales for big savings. Just remember where you hid them.

Impulse Spending

No amount of me telling you to spend less will work when it comes up against a desire to buy-buy-buy. Impulse spending is when we purchase something without thinking. We don't act on our common sense. It can range from candy in the checkout line to an upscale motor home, boat, or mountain retreat. These are the kinds of purchases that give you two highs. The first high is when you purchase it and the second high is when you sell it (usually at a loss). The impulsive purchase comes at you without you thinking it through.

Understand that you are fooling yourself by telling yourself it's something you always wanted. You did not always want it. You probably didn't want it six months ago, or maybe not even until a very gifted salesperson starting raving about it. Or you might tell yourself that you deserve it. Maybe you do; you still shouldn't buy it. Everything you tell yourself is all a rationalization to be impulsive, to let yourself off the hook.

You are reading this book because you want to be wealthy. Buying a snazzy new car won't make you wealthy. Those extra car payments will take away from money that could be spent building your future. (I know, this is my refrain, but I keep saying it because it's true.) If your current vehicle is no longer safe to drive, what can you afford? Which cars are affordable and would serve your needs (rather than your wants)? Could you buy a used car?

Even the boat or mountain home could reasonably be enjoyed by renting rather than buying. Then you can see how much you actually like living in the mountains, or whether you are prone to seasickness. Impulse buyers don't even think of how useful the purchase will be, and rarely think of related expenses (mooring, travel, insurance, fuel costs, just to name a few). They just want the high of buying it or of playing one-upmanship with their relatives, friends, and neighbors.

Go instead for the high of closing your next deal or of taking your business to the next level. Let other people take pleasure in the false belief that their impulse really makes them better. Conspicuous consumption can burn a hole in your budget, while holding back and rethinking can save you a lot of trouble financially. If you have a problem with impulse buying, get help.

Having talked at length about the virtues of being frugal, I'm now going to tell you a story about something big that I bought, not frugally at all. I picked one thing that, to me, meant success and I let myself have that. Not right away, not while I was building my investment nest egg, but after I had bought multiple properties and finally had a steadily growing income from my real estate investments, my various counseling services, investment advising, and the rest of my side income, which always made the difference for us financially. Here's how it happened.

My wife, Bernice, and I had been socking away money for years and using it to buy apartment buildings (I'll go into the how-to in a later chapter), and one day, when I was doing the books, I realized that we had finally hit an annual income of $1 million. It had kind of snuck up on us—we were so busy doing the work, managing the apartments, taking care of business and our kids. My whole life up to that point, I had driven a clunker of a car. That month, I splurged and bought my first Jaguar. It was a mark of my achievement, of how far I'd come. It was not an impulse buy, and it was very, very satisfying.

You can do that now, today. Not the buying part, but deciding what you will buy and when you will buy it. Where are the goalposts? What is the big milestone that you want to reach on your path to success? Now decide how you will reward yourself when you get there. It can be an experience or a thing, but it should be meaningful to you. Whenever you think about buying something on impulse, measure it against that big prize that's waiting for you. Is it worth trading your dream purchase for a pair of expensive shoes or a motorcycle you'll only ride on weekends? Stay focused and keep your eye on the real prize.

Chapter Four

Smart Spenders and Savers

I'm going to stick with the theme of buying for a little while longer, because of course you will buy things: food, clothing, necessities, and luxuries. The key to being a smart spender is knowing *how* to buy. The first step when purchasing something is to do a little research and understand when the right time is to buy something. The three key criteria are quality, price, and need.

Quality

Virtually everything you buy has a time frame of how long it will last. Something as simple as bed sheets have a thread count that determines the quality and wear of the sheets. Even the way shirts are made and how strong the stitching is can determine the lifespan of the shirt. Different manufacturers have their own quality standards.

You never want to get sucked into buying something cheap. For example, cheap clothes notoriously don't last as long as well-made ones. You will spend more over the course of a few years—a lot more—on buying and replacing poorly made, inexpensive clothes, shoes, furniture, and appliances. You have two options when it comes to buying quality: You can plan your purchases and be very deliberate about a few high-quality items, or you can buy good things secondhand.

Here's an example: If you work anywhere in the business world, whether you are a man or a woman, you will need one good business suit. You can put money aside and not buy other things, maybe work part-time for a little extra spending money, and buy a new, high-quality suit, tailored to fit. That works. You will have it for years, can wear it with different blouses or shirts, and you will always look professional. Or you can visit some consignment stores where you can find high-quality wear at half the price. Even thrift stores and yard sales can be shopped with discretion. Don't get sucked into buying something just because it's cheap and you're desperate. Again, planning in advance what you will need takes the pressure off and can help prevent impulsive buys. But people get rid of perfectly good clothes because they are Marie Kondo-ing their closets, have lost or gained weight, or have retired or changed careers. Small imperfections, like missing buttons, falling hems, or an imperfect fit, can be expertly fixed by a tailor (many dry cleaners offer alterations as well).

This strategy will cost you time as you devote Saturday mornings to "thrifting," but it can save you the equivalent of a part-time job—assuming you can stop yourself from buying junk. Only buy quality, and keep a list of what you need. This is an especially good idea if you are fitting out your first apartment in addition to your business wardrobe. Look for beautiful things that will serve you well for a long time and resist buying other people's tchotchkes.

Price

When evaluating the cost of similar products, be aware that the prices may be attributable to the content of the product not being the same—not just in terms of quality, but quantity as well. An example of this is a cereal box. The volume of cereal in the box varies from brand to brand. Some companies will charge more for less product if the demand is greater. When making these purchases, you have to ask yourself what the reason behind the price difference might be.

Personally, I love this. I love thinking about what makes someone put a certain price on, well, anything. To me, it's a game, and I gain an understanding of so much else when I stop to think about the factors that go into it. There's marketing, creating a desire for a product. Sometimes, a higher price makes something seem more valuable than the sum of its parts. There's convenience; it always costs more to have someone else take care of a problem than to do it yourself. Even instant, single-serve packets of oatmeal are, meal for meal, more expensive than the regular kind you need to cook.

When you look at a price tag, look beyond the raw numbers and figure out what you're really paying for. You'll feel smart because you'll be smart—you'll learn so much about marketing, supply and demand, even psychology. These will all serve you well in your own business career. Above all, you'll put yourself in a position to make good decisions about what you're willing to pay for and when to save your hard-earned money for a better buy.

Need

It's not just what you can afford, but what you need. And I mean "need" as in an actual need as an adult human being, not an "I need that!" like a kid in a toy store. You really don't need as much as you think you do. There are plenty of people who don't need to buy lunch every day, for instance, because they could pack it. Yes, you need food. No, dinner doesn't need to be ordered in every night.

Making deliberate purchases instead of impulse buys is key to building wealth. It's also environmentally responsible. The huge amount of trash and yard sales and the need for storage facilities all speak to the waste in our economy. And don't just think in the abstract about all the money you'll save by cutting out impulse buys. Actually track it. Each day, write down what you didn't get and how much you saved—in after-tax dollars! That money represents hours of your life that you trade for dollars. When you think of it that way, you are trading your life for a new toaster. It is clearly worth the time and effort to build the habit of resisting impulse buys.

This may sound counterintuitive, but when thinking about buying something, you should NEVER ask yourself, "Do I need it?" That question is a trap. Your brain will trick you nine times out of ten. It will create all sorts of scenarios in which you *may* need or *could* need or (most insidious of all) *deserve* the thing. So don't bother asking a question that will only elicit useless answers. Instead, ask yourself, "Can I live without it?"

Can you manage without the intended purchase? Most of the time, yes, you can. And by asking yourself that question, your brain will start thinking of what you could do instead. In fact, that's a terrific follow-up question: "What can I use that I already have?" Even better, I want you to picture yourself using the money you would spend on the thing—whatever the thing is—to build your business, to get you out of a jam six months from now, to invest in yourself. Spending wisely isn't about never spending money. It's about having it there to be spent when you need it to build your future. That is the perfect time to spend it, when the answer is that you can't manage without it. This is almost never for the purchase of a "thing." It's for the building of a prototype or the funding of a business or the purchase of a rental property, or for an emergency fund. Something that will let you leverage the money into real wealth.

Free Fun

Here's another great game to play: What can I do that's fun and free? Once you start looking, you'll find there's no end to the fun you can have for little to no money. Walk in the park, go to state beaches, hike camping trails, attend free outdoor concerts, check out local parades and street fairs, take advantage of school and church programs, and visit your library for books, videos, and lectures.

I'm not telling you to hole up at home and watch free TV every night (although I'm not saying that shouldn't be an option!). What I am telling you is this:

- It's not necessary to go to an event that carries an exorbitant price tag when you can get the same amount of fun for next to nothing. Most costly entertainment is largely heavy marketing that plays into our fears of missing out or our desire to be part of the "in" crowd. That stuff is all in your head. Before you buy an expensive ticket, look at why you want to go. Is it to impress someone—a date or your friends, or even yourself? Think about it: Wouldn't you be more impressive with a million-dollar business in five or ten years than with a $40 T-shirt from some concert?

- Rather than being pulled into costly entertainment as a spectator, it can be more rewarding to be a participant. Instead of going to a comedy night, why not take a class in improv? Instead of going to "foodie" restaurants, take a gourmet cooking class, or learn about wines. If you already have a hobby, you can double down on it by taking a free online course or going to a meetup with other people who are equally passionate. In addition to the fun of taking the class itself, you'll be rewarded with greater expertise and new social connections—both of which can enhance your business as well as your life.

At the risk of hitting this too hard, I really want you to consider that there are hundreds of things you can fully enjoy that cost little to nothing in terms of money. Local colleges, libraries, churches, and community centers often host free or low-cost musical events, art galleries, lecture series, and theater. Matinee movies and happy hours provide the same experience for less money; the only difference is the time of day. And getting together with friends over a potluck rather than at a pricey restaurant saves you money and buys you a relaxed atmosphere.

It really is a decision about priorities. If your priority is to be financially secure, then being deliberate about where and how you spend money—and creative about finding fun, free ways to live your best life—is the most important choice you can make.

Saving Money

There is nothing boring about saving money. To see a savings account grow gives you peace of mind knowing you're prepared not just for emergencies, but also for adventure. You can save for a vacation and know the vacation did not put you into debt. You can have a great idea for a business or an unexpected opportunity and have the resources to jump into it. You can tell when a person has a "nest egg" because they are free to take advantage of whatever comes their way without fear. The ultimate saver is the person who saves for their own peace of mind, because when you don't have to play it safe, you can play big.

I speak from experience. When my late wife, Bernice, and I were first married, we took a lot of evening strolls in the park, watched a lot of TV, and ate at home almost exclusively. We lived off of her salary while I went to college, and then lived off of mine when I had my degree and we started a family. But we did more than just live on either salary; we saved on it as well—enough that we were able to take financial risks. We mitigated those risks by, for instance, purchasing an eight-unit apartment complex so that if we couldn't make our own mortgage, we could sell our house and live in one of our apartments.

I always recommend having a backup plan to make sure you and your family don't end up on the street. But I also urgently recommend saving, no matter how little you currently make, so that you can have money to build on later. Saving is a path to riches.

Chapter Five

Investing in Yourself

Over the course of your lifetime, your workplace earnings are going to be the biggest source of your wealth. Not just because of the money you directly make from working, but because of how you leverage this money in order to make more money, either through stocks or real estate or your own business. Unless you have inherited wealth or family wealth, the basis for everything you do is the money you earn—and save. So let's talk about your career.

When you are just starting out, the work you do can be thought of as your apprenticeship. This is the job that teaches you how to work, as well as how to work specifically in your field. Some skills are transferable, while some, such as learning a particular software, are industry-specific. This first job is what gets you started, but it is not your ultimate goal. Yet that doesn't mean it can't have a tremendous impact on where you end up.

Your first several jobs will influence your career in so many ways: They will lay the foundation of your understanding of the industry, provide you with the skills and experience you need to make you a good candidate for a better job, and shape your network of people on whom you can rely to help you succeed in this and other jobs. That is why it's important for your early jobs to support your career. There's nothing wrong with flipping burgers for extra cash, but that is not how you lay a foundation for your career. Don't get stuck in a dead-end job; use it to create your emergency cushion or support you while you finish your education, but always be looking for a job that will teach you something you can parlay into something better.

Moving forward, I'm going to replace the word "job" with the word "work." I prefer to talk about your work, because it's unsettling to think that you have a job and not to think you have to work. Even in the lowliest position, you should still be working as hard as you can. I am a firm believer that my work has value for the pay I receive. And working beyond others' expectations of you is, unfortunately, so rare that it will always make you stand out.

So how can you make your work support your career? There are three important things to think about no matter where you are:

- What can you learn about your industry? Look not just at your own work, but also at your workplace and the larger organization. Look at the big picture: What is the goal of the company? The goal of your department? How about the industry as a whole? On a practical level, how can you learn more? What are the trade publications/websites that everyone reads? Who is seen as a top figure, i.e., the Warren Buffet or Steve Jobs or Oprah of your particular niche? What kind of temperament or ability is valued?

- What skills can you learn? What skills do the people above you have? What about people in the next department over? How can you be of greater value? What kind of experience do you need to develop personal skills, such as negotiation techniques or handling clients or making sales? Is there someone you could shadow or offer to help on a project that would give you experience in something beyond your current day-to-day?

- Network. With everyone. This isn't about shaking hands and doling out business cards, it's about making a personal connection. Get along with everyone at work. Take supervision gracefully. Don't antagonize anyone. When you're good at something, don't rub it in; show your ability artfully. Build a network of people by helping them and by being genuinely friendly and interested in their work.

As you succeed with your first employer and go from being an "apprentice" to being more of a "journeyman," you may discover that you have gone as far as you can. At this point, it's time to explore other job opportunities. As you develop experience, skill, and contacts, you can use all of those things to create greater financial opportunity. It could be time to look for a move, either within the organization or outside of it, that will give you a higher pay grade.

When you see opportunity, take it. It could be anything from changing departments to changing employers. How do you know an opportunity when you see one? You want a place where you can put your current skills to work in a slightly different way, where you can learn new skills, and where you can meet new people who will give you an alternate perspective and increase the value of both your understanding and your network. Moving out of your comfort zone allows you to cross-pollinate, bringing your own ideas and abilities into a new situation and broadening your horizons. It can also help you to avoid boredom and meet new challenges.

I truly believe that no matter where your finances are, real wealth lies in the ability to make decisions without fearing that a choice could leave you destitute. Back when I was working for other people, I was able to quit jobs that no longer worked for me without fear because I had confidence in both my own abilities and in my strong network of people I knew or had helped or who held me in high esteem. I knew I would always be able to find another full-time job, and even if it took a little while (it never did), I could double down on my side business and always have some reliable income. Get good at what you do, be honest and kind to people, and have at least a second income stream. These things won't just set you up to make money—they will create real wealth by keeping you from becoming trapped in a bad job or situation.

Hard Work

My attitude has always been to work hard. I wanted to do more than what was asked of me in every situation. When working for the Department of Corporations as an examiner, I was given a boring assignment that my supervisor had already done once before with his three examiners only a year prior. It took a total of four months for their team of four people to complete it. When I was given the assignment, only two other examiners were assigned to this project with me. I told my coworkers we were going to do better than the team before us, despite the fact that we had fewer people. We finished that project in two months—half the time! And we were excited by it, not bored in the least, because we had created for ourselves a reason to roll up our sleeves and get to work. Our accomplishment was tremendously rewarding.

This is only one of the benefits of hard work. It brings so much gratification to do more than is expected. It's just not job security; it actually feels good to be effective and it can create a bond between team members. But another benefit is that others notice it, too. Hard work helps you to accomplish more and gets you noticed. This increases your value to the company and the career opportunities they might be able to offer you.

Everything I know about working hard and driving myself came from my mom. She worked all the time and built a better future for us on the foundation of sewing piecework—usually a subsistence job at best. I made it my goal while working for someone else to give my employer their money's worth, every time. When I went out on my own, I kept the same work ethic and it has always paid off.

Supplemental Income

Early on in life, you have an abundant amount of energy. Why not use it? When I was younger, I used my extra energy to provide supplemental income over and above my regular salary. Nowadays, we call it a "side hustle," but at the time, I just called it using my skills to the fullest. When I worked for the IRS, I ran my own company in my spare time advising people on their taxes. It was entirely ethical (and fully reported on my income tax!), and I truly enjoyed using my free time to provide advice on how to legally use the Internal Revenue code to limit one's tax liability. It wasn't long before I had a steady clientele who would often refer me to their friends. I had as much work as I could handle, and as a journeyman-level agent in the IRS, I found myself making more than the L.A. Director. That felt pretty good, too!

Later, as I succeeded in real estate opportunities, I built a secondary business using my real estate savvy to advise my clients and evaluate property they were considering. The commission paid was welcome income, and I used the information I learned by working for a variety of people on investments I wouldn't have thought of to guide my own investments.

Never be reliant on a sole source of income. The days when you could trust a company to take care of you from high school to the grave are long past—if, in fact, they were ever really there. Just as you can't gamble your retirement funds on a single stock, you need to hedge against possible career setbacks (getting laid off, being passed over for advancement, pay cuts, or even your employer going out of business) by having other income. Additionally, other sources of employment will open up new career possibilities you never thought of.

A second stream of income is also important because it gives you the ability to save and invest. When my late wife, Bernice, and I were starting out, we had a rule in our household: Money made from second jobs was used for investments. And we kept to it, even when the kids started coming, even when money was tight, because the satisfaction we got from seeing our investments grow couldn't be matched by a night out on the town. Plus, it kept us from being wasteful with our salaried income. We always looked at that extra income as our future—it was icing on the cake, but definitely not icing to be enjoyed now.

I know I touched on this earlier, but it's worth repeating: People think that saving money equals depriving themselves—and if you think of it that way, you will never save enough money to leverage a big deal or invest in your own business. Happily, nothing could be further from the truth.

First of all, you will always have as much fun as you decide to have. You can be miserable on a tropical beach or having a blast at a free concert in the park. Local museums often have admission-free Sundays, community groups have workshops and gatherings, and volunteer organizations offer a way to do good while getting together with like-minded people and making friends. There are a million ways to enjoy yourself without spending money; use your creativity and try them out until you find what you truly love.

But even more importantly, experiencing the joy of using your vision and resources to create more opportunity for yourself and your family is what's really invigorating—that's what makes life worth living. You always need to have something to strive for. Sitting around and being a couch potato will shorten your life, both in terms of the number of days and the amount of joy.

Jealousy

Unfortunately, as you improve your standard of living, education, or accomplishments, someone is probably going to become jealous of you. Usually it's someone close to you. This can be very disturbing. How do you cope?

First, you have to not let them affect you. They are insecure about losing you and being upstaged by your accomplishments. Second, see this as an opportunity to share with them. Possibly they want to succeed as well, but are at a loss as to how to do it. Provide them with your steps for success. Explain the challenges and effort it took to reach your goal. Give them something to do for themselves. They may not listen, but you will know that you've done what you could. For me, writing this book is one way I'm trying to help by showing you what worked for me.

Personally, I was naïve. When friends expressed envy, my first thought was always "My goodness, buddy, you can do this, too! There's no reason to envy me." I would always say, "Let me show you how it's done." I'd try to coax them along. I remember three guys in my office when I worked for the IRS all following my lead and investing in income property. The problem was they didn't have the energy or really the desire to run a business on top of their day job. They'd rather work for someone else. So they never stopped being jealous, even though it was their decision not to pursue a side business.

I tried to eliminate envy, and I'm sorry to tell you that you can't, at least not completely. You can show them how it's done and be a mentor, but understand that it's not for everyone. The best you can do is relieve your own angst by trying to bring them in. Stay humble. Have a plan to cope. And know that if they can't walk through the door you're holding open for them, it's not about you. You've done your part.

Naysayers

We are surrounded by naysayers. These are the people who sound like they're the voice of reason, but really, all they're doing is holding you back. Sometimes they have their own agenda, sometimes they are simply afraid for you, and sometimes they just don't understand. You can provide more information, you can explain your reasoning, and you should definitely use their comments to sharpen your own thoughts. That's a gift they give you, if you can look at their objections and see if any are valid and can be incorporated into your game plan without getting caught up in the drama. But in the final analysis, you need to move on.

In general, naysayers are negative people and are short on progress. It is the optimist who has imagination, takes risks, and accomplishes miracles.

Value

It's important for you to discover what a good life means to you. You do this not only by filling your life with work you enjoy and feel proud of, but also by determining what you truly value and following that path.

There are things we say we value, but the way you know that you do value something is that you choose it. You create it. You can build a life that aligns with your values by using your creative instincts and exploration. Value comes from the things we create, produce, and spend time on, and even the things we think.

The opportunities for creativity are endless. Nothing ever needs to be as it is right now. Got a better way to invoice customers? Try it out. Come up with a solution to a problem? See if there's a way to solve it for the masses. Write a book. Teach a workshop or a webinar. Just as an artist can use a blank canvas and some paints to create a masterpiece that becomes invaluable, so, too, can you use your talents to unlock answers to the questions that absorb you. And in doing so, you can potentially help or inspire others.

We all gain from a promising future, and that future lies in our own creation of value. Your journey will be richer for your active participation in building a life that aligns with what you stand for. It reminds me of a story about a man visiting a construction site to see several workers at work. As he approached the first worker, he asked him, "What are you doing?"

The man replied, "I dig up rocks from the quarry and bring the rocks to the next worker."

The visitor went to the next worker and asked him what he was doing.

The worker said, "I shape the rocks into squares."

The visitor continued and asked the third worker what he was doing.

This man replied: "I am building a cathedral."

Chapter Six

Owning Your Own Home

Owning your own home is a cornerstone of the American Dream, and for good reason. Your home purchase is a good way to build an estate. Home prices have generally increased, although as we've seen, sudden drops in the economy can hurt your resale in the short-term—a good reminder to not wait until you absolutely need the money to liquidate any asset. I'll talk a little more about that later.

But generally speaking, your home appreciates in value, and once the mortgage is paid off, it can leave you with both a comfortable, rent-free place to live (although property taxes and insurance remain) and a nest egg in retirement. But purchasing your own home isn't just good for the future: It's good for now. Owning your home gives you stability and a sense of roots. It gives you the ability to pick the neighborhood you wish to live and raise your children in without worrying about increases in rent or the whims of a landlord. And let's not forget the freedom of how you either decorate or improve.

Home ownership is also good for society in general. By and large, people take better care of a place they own than they do a place they rent. We invest in an area emotionally as well as financially when we call it home. And as individuals, we benefit from the sense of security and belonging that comes from putting down roots.

All of that said, home ownership is a big decision, and for many the biggest single investment they will make. Don't take it lightly. Really think about what kind of life your home purchase will make possible. The house itself matters, of course, but even more important than that is the neighborhood. What's the school district like? How far is your commute? What about grocery stores and libraries? What's the public transportation like? Where's the closest fire station? (This can make a difference in your homeowner's insurance as well.) Are your healthcare professionals—doctor, dentist, eye doctor—still close by, or will you have to find a whole new team?

These are questions you should ask yourself no matter who you are. But there are other questions you need to ask depending on your own particular needs. For example, if you have small children, are there safe parks with playgrounds? I know a woman whose mother had Alzheimer's; when her mother was moving in with her, she needed a neighborhood with little traffic and lots of sidewalks, ideally on a cul-de-sac, where it would be safer for her mother to walk during her roaming phase. While you can't control everything, you need to think deeply about your needs and even rank them so you'll know what you can compromise on and what is really nonnegotiable.

When you're looking at the house itself, there are numerous things to take into consideration. I never recommend that you go for either the worst or the best house on a block or neighborhood. The worst house may require more updating than you expected, while the cost of the best house may never be recouped. Go to a lot of open houses so you can see what you like and don't like about different floor plans.

You should also be thinking about the future. You may not have children now, but are you planning to? I'm not saying you need a five-bedroom home right out of the gate, but you should always be able to imagine yourself someplace for at least a decade. An extra bedroom now could become either a nursery or a home office if you start your own business.

Start by figuring out where you want to live to lead the life you want to have. Next, you'll figure out how to pay for it.

Home Loans

You might want to start looking for the money to pay for the house before you start looking for the house itself. As with everything, having your ducks in a row in advance is a good idea. It's easier to have a calm head with a thought-out budget before your heart is sold on the idea. Everything in life, including buying a home, has to be a combination of both heart and head.

Start by checking with as many lenders as possible for the best terms and conditions. Get preapproved; what are they offering you? This will also help you resolve any problems that come to light. Maybe you need to save more for your down payment. Maybe you need to clean up your credit score. If something is going to stop your home purchase in its tracks, it's far better to know now than when you're trying to make an offer.

Once you've talked to several lenders and found the best deal for you, it's time to negotiate. Start with the stated terms and then see what can be adjusted. Where are they willing to bend a little? For instance, sometimes you can get money for a home improvement in the same loan as the mortgage if they hold that money in escrow until the improvement is completed.

It's also important to build a relationship with the person—the actual person, not the institution—giving you the loan. When you're shopping for your loan, pay attention to who you connect with, who is competent and approachable. See what other business of yours you can give them now, however small. Refer them to other people. Once you do get a loan from them (assuming all goes well), maintain the relationship. Going back to the same people for your business loans and other real estate loans can lay a foundation of trust so that when you need something—an extension, a quick turnaround, payment flexibility—you're not trying to convince a stranger; you're working together with a friend.

Negotiating

Negotiating is a skill you will use your whole life. I'm going to talk about it here in the context of home buying, but I want you to understand that negotiation itself is a tremendous life skill. It's worth investing in learning negotiation techniques and practicing deliberately every chance you get. Most people need to get over their fear of negotiating. Seeing it as a win-win definitely helps. Think of the other person not as your opponent, but as your ally; together, you're trying to make something work. Solving the situation to everyone's advantage is always the goal.

Let's look at how this can play out when you're buying a home. Once you have your ballpark of how much you can afford, you need to be on the lookout for the right home at the right price. There are a lot of things to consider. First, there's the market price. You should know going in what comparable houses have sold for (not their asking prices, but their sales prices), and then expect the seller to be asking for a little over that. This is where your negotiating skills come in.

To begin with, the seller usually leaves some room at the top. They start a little high, giving them some leeway to reduce the price. Of course, if you don't ask for it, you don't get it. You should always ask for a reduction in the sales price. Yes, sometimes there are bidding wars on a particular house. I recommend you don't get involved in those. Just like bidding at an auction, people sometimes allow their competitive spirit to overtake their common sense. There are plenty of houses that will suit your needs. Decide before you go into your home search how much you're willing to spend. You should be prepared to walk away rather than go beyond a certain level.

Next, see if the seller can give you any perks, such as termite clearance, allowance for painting, deferred maintenance, even a new roof. These things can justify going a little higher with your bid, since you would have to pay for them anyway. Also see if the closing date of the purchase suits you; you may have other financial commitments. A little extra time may open up enough money for you to complete the purchase and make everyone happy.

Again, negotiations are about working together, not about beating the other person. Have a list of things you're prepared to offer, and be creative in what they might be.

I'll give you an example from my own life—not a house negotiation, but a business one. I was the third partner in a restaurant deal and I knew the other two didn't want to give me a stake in the restaurant itself. In fact, I didn't want a stake in the restaurant. Restaurants are a risky business! Instead, I offered to take a one-third stake in the land they purchased for the restaurant. They were happy and I was happy; they got to keep the restaurant just between the two of them, and I got part ownership in land that I knew would appreciate faster than the business. We were all able to have our needs met and we all won from the deal.

In a real estate situation, think about what you might have to offer. Can you be flexible about the settlement date? Can you offer them an extra month or two where you rent the house back to them so their kids can finish the school year at their current school? If you have the flexibility to buy the house without it being contingent on the sale of your current house, that can be attractive to a seller; no one wants a sale to fall out of escrow because the buyer couldn't sell their own home in time. (On a related note, it's extremely important for you to have a contingency in your closing to extend the date if you haven't been able to sell your own home. I've seen people suddenly burdened with two mortgages and forced to sell their old home at any price. Be smart. Don't let that happen to you.)

If you find yourself working with someone who won't give on any issue, be willing to walk away from the deal. Someone playing hardball isn't someone who is going to help you solve problems now or if something comes up later—in the home inspection, for example. Once, on a rental property I wanted, the seller went with an offer that was more than I wanted to pay. That was fine, it was his prerogative. It helps in business to not take things personally; you want to keep the door open if you can for future deals. A couple of months later, the seller called me, asking if I was still interested. I told him sure, but only at my original price. He agreed! Turns out that the buyer who outbid me was manipulating everything about the property that you can imagine. He was relentlessly trying to change the deal in escrow. The seller finally had enough; he walked away. "I would rather get less with you," he told me, "but be sure of what I'm getting." Which is a lesson in itself: Always be fair and stand by your word. You'll get a reputation for integrity that will help you get what you want down the line. People want to work with someone whose word is good.

Investment

Thinking about your home purchase as an investment means that you are always looking for ways to make the best use of your home's value. This means viewing each part of your property, inside and outside, for possible improvements.

- Unused space in areas such as attics, basements, or garages can be made into usable space of one kind or another. Be sure to get permits!

- Kitchen and bathrooms can be remodeled with new fixtures.

- Updating décor in any room is helpful.

- Landscaping with flowering plants will add beauty to your home.

It's not just when you plan to sell that your home's value matters. If your home increases in appraised value, it means you can borrow on the equity that's built up. Ask anyone who knows me—I'm relentless when it comes to fixing up my home and my investment properties. I am always looking for ways to increase value (and in investment properties, this doesn't just lead to being able to charge more rent, but also to attract and retain tenants who value maintaining a beautiful property). A few years after fixing up my house, I was able to use the equity that had built up to make a rental property investment that provided even greater return. Everything you do is a stepping stone for the next thing you're going to do.

Leverage

For many people, buying their own home is the largest purchase they will ever make. Aside from getting the best price for the home they want, the actual terms of the mortgage loan are important, too. Mortgage is leverage. You can only buy so much with your own money. Rarely can you buy a house with cash on hand—and you shouldn't. Leverage minimizes your down payment in case you made a wrong purchase—which happens.

Leverage is sometimes referred to as "other people's money," or OPM. Leveraging is when you use outside funds to:

- Maximize cash flow

- Improve your ability to control more assets

- Limit your exposure to risk

An example of leverage that's most often used is in buying a home, although I've also used it to great advantage in buying investment properties, which I'll talk more about in a bit. Please take a look at the table on the following page for a leverage example for a 30-year loan at 3.5% when the value of the home increased by 2.5%.

Let me explain what you're looking at. In the first example, you purchase a home valued at $340,000 with a down payment of $34,000. Over the years, your principal left on the loan will decrease, because you're paying a little off every month. At the same time, the home's value is increasing. So, the equity in your house is, at first, just equal to your down payment, but over time, it appreciates not just by the amount you've paid off, but also by the amount the house has appreciated.

Here's why there are two examples: I want you to see how much more equity you can get for a little extra money up front and a slightly higher monthly mortgage. This is important because the equity in your home can be your biggest financial resource to leverage down the road.

LEVERAGE EXAMPLE FOR A 30-YEAR LOAN AT 3.5% WHEN THE VALUE OF THE HOME INCREASES BY 2.5%

EXAMPLE 1

	HOME VALUE	DOWN PAYMENT	INFLATION	LOAN BALANCE	EQUITY
AFTER 1 YEAR	$340,000	$34,000	$8,500	DECREASING	$42,500
AFTER 10 YEARS	$425,000		$85,000	DECREASING	
AFTER 20 YEARS	$510,000		$170,000	DECREASING	
AFTER 30 YEARS	$595,000		$255,000	$0	$595,000

EXAMPLE 2

	HOME VALUE	DOWN PAYMENT	INFLATION	LOAN BALANCE	EQUITY
AFTER 1 YEAR	$540,000	$50,000	$13,500	DECREASING	$63,500
AFTER 10 YEARS	$675,000		$135,000	DECREASING	
AFTER 20 YEARS	$810,000		$270,000	DECREASING	
AFTER 30 YEARS	$945,000		$405,000	$0	$945,000

In Example 2, for just $16,000 more as a down payment, you can leverage into twice the equity in thirty years. I know it's a long time, but what a difference this could make to your life! It's much easier to stretch with the right budget. Why wouldn't you want to buy the more expensive house? Yes, your payments are higher, but if you can make that happen, look what happens in five, ten, or twenty years in terms of the money you now have available to leverage.

Let me also explain what home ownership is: Until you pay off that mortgage, it's the bank that owns your house because the bank lent you the money to purchase the house. It owns the mortgage. Here's another way to think about it: Your home is collateral against the loan you took out to buy it. So if you don't pay your mortgage, the bank can take possession of your house. This is something you want to avoid! This is why you set aside emergency funds and you have a plan. If something happens and the economy tanks (and we've all lived through that from time to time), or if your company is sold and you lose your job, what else could you do to make sure that you and your family are, at a minimum, eating and paying your mortgage?

I always had backup money in my budget. First, I almost always had what is now known as a side hustle going on, such as giving tax advice, which I mentioned earlier. But my own small consulting business wasn't my only backup plan. When my late wife, Bernice, and I bought our first apartment building, it was a financial stretch. I figured, why buy a three- or four-unit building when we could swing an eight-unit building? It was roughly the same amount of work for twice the benefits and, again, a little more slack: If one unit remained unrented, that was one-quarter of the income of a smaller building, but only one-eighth of the potential income of a larger building. Pro tip: Always do the math!

At first, Bernice was not quite as enthusiastic as I was to buy the bigger building. She told me I couldn't afford it; I told her to watch me make it happen. And I did. But that didn't mean I was reckless. As I mentioned earlier, my backup plan was to move the entire family into one of our own units and sell the house if I had to. I loved our house, so it wouldn't have been an ideal solution, but we wouldn't have lost our investment and my family would not have been without a roof over their heads. In fact, we didn't need to sell the house; we were able to start making money almost right away. I chose a good property—which I'll go into a little bit later—and we worked as a family to improve the landscape, paint and clean the apartments, and make it a welcoming place to live. But I did have that safety net in the back of my mind.

You should have a safety net in the back of your mind as well. To keep your house, could you rent out a room? Could you move in with family for a year and rent out your entire house? When I was transferred from New York City to Charlotte, North Carolina, early in my career, I lived in a YMCA for a couple of weeks until someone told me about a place offering room and board. For $12/week, I had my own room and regular meals. I could sleep there, eat breakfast, make my own lunch, and then be fed dinner. The woman who ran it supported both herself and her chronically unemployed husband. She had four boarders total, and she was able to do well: keep her house, drive a decent car, live a comfortable life despite a partner who didn't chip in. It was a good deal for everyone. She used her head to make the best of a bad situation and didn't have to starve. When you're industrious, you will find a way.

It's worth spending the time to really think about your home as an investment, rather than only thinking of it as the place where you live. Consider this: You are leveraging the small(er) amount of money that you are taking from other assets (savings and investments) and borrowing someone else's money (this is the mortgage) to parlay your initial investment into a property. You choose to live in that property rather than rent it out, but it's still a real estate investment. It appreciates over time.

Another important aspect when buying a home is making sure the mortgage terms are suitable for your payments. Be smart about both the value of the property you are buying and the terms of your deal. How much are you paying to borrow money? The interest and points on your loan are the cost of borrowing. A lower interest rate on the loan doesn't just mean a lower monthly payment for you, but also a lower investment of funds on your end overall, over the life of the loan. Which means when you sell, you'll make more profit in the long run.

Also, just by adding a few dollars to each payment, you can reduce your principal quickly. For the first fifteen years, most of your payment goes toward the interest, so putting in a little extra to pay down the principal is a good use of your savings. An accelerated monthly payment can also decrease the amount of time you'll be paying interest, which, again, decreases the total amount you spend on the mortgage (look for and be wary of any penalties for paying the loan off early). You always want to look for ways to make the most of your investment.

Insurance for Your Home

Here's a cost no one thinks about when they buy their first home, so be prepared: insurance. There are three different kinds of insurance policies you may need, and some of them sound similar.

The first is homeowners insurance to cover fire and liability. This is critical whether you have a mortgage or not (would you really be willing to let a fire wipe out the lifetime of equity you built up in your home?), but it is also usually required by your lender while they hold the mortgage on your house. When you are thinking about how much you can afford to pay each month for your mortgage (which has a direct impact on how much money you can borrow), you need to factor in how much you'll be paying for homeowners insurance. You may already be paying renters insurance, and if so, talk to your agent about how much more homeowners insurance would be for the kind of property you are planning to buy. Shop around and get a few quotes; this should give you a ballpark figure. These are the kinds of hidden costs you don't want to be surprised by after you've gone into escrow.

Next is private mortgage insurance (PMI). PMI is required by most lenders if your down payment is less than 20 percent of the purchase price of your home. It covers your loan; it doesn't cover your house. Let's put in some possible numbers: If you're looking a $500,000 home, you may need to put in $100,000 or more as a down payment to avoid having to pay for PMI. You will keep paying the PMI until you have paid off enough of your loan to reach that 20 percent investment threshold. Again, this is something you need to factor in before you sign.

The third form of insurance is not required, but many choose to add it, and that's mortgage protection insurance (MPI). Not to be confused with PMI, MPI is actually a form of life insurance that insures the loan on your home if you were to die. It's generally a term insurance, meaning it's only good for a certain number of years. Premiums and terms vary widely, but if this is something that will give you peace of mind, it may be worth looking into. It doesn't take the place of life insurance, which would protect your beneficiary should you die. But this type of term insurance would take care of the mortgage, for an annual premium. Make sure the term will cover the entire length of the mortgage. I always had mortgage insurance on every property I owned. For me, the premium was worth the peace of mind knowing that if I had died before the loan balance was paid off, my family would at least have their home free and clear. I wouldn't have stuck them with a loan on top of their grief.

Home Equity Loan

If the value of your home exceeds your loan balance, the difference between the two is your home equity. For instance, using Example 2 in the chart we saw earlier, let's say you bought your house for $540,000 with $50,000 down. Your loan is $490,000 and your home's value is $540,000. Your equity in the house is $50,000. Pretty straightforward, right?

Fast forward ten years. Your mortgage is down to about $380,000 and your home's value has increased to $675,000. (Obviously, this is an example and I'm keeping the numbers simple, but it's in the ballpark.) Now the equity in your home is the difference between $675,000 and $380,000; that's $295,000 in equity, up from $50,000 in just ten years.

You might want to tap into that money.

Home equity can be a great source of funds for smart investing—investing in yourself, a new business, an income-generating property. A home equity loan is a second lien on your property. You can also use it to remodel your home or, if you're in real bind, pay off credit cards, which accrue interest at a much higher rate.

It's probably worth noting again that I'm not a fan of credit cards. Pay them off every month or only use them in an emergency. The interest rates, penalties, and fees can be a stone around your neck, both in terms of crippling monthly payments and dings to your credit score that can prevent you from moving forward on bigger, better investments. If you live on less than you earn every month, you can avoid falling into the credit card trap, and that is real freedom.

Home Equity Conversion Mortgage or Reverse Mortgage

Finally, a home equity conversion mortgage (HECM) is a type of mortgage loan that the Federal Housing Administration (FHA) funds. The loan is available only to homeowners age sixty-two and older. The loan does not become due for as long as the homeowner lives in the property as their primary residence. There isn't a monthly loan payment. Owners are responsible for property taxes, insurance, and maintenance on the property. The FHA can allow up to $700,000 for your loan. Each year this figure is evaluated by the FHA and it increases year to year. It's not for everyone, but if you are older and you need to access the equity in your house, not having a monthly loan payment can be very attractive.

Disclaimer

As with all the advice I give in this book, do your own due diligence. Some investments are right for some people and not for others; the same is true of loans, of insurance, of every possible decision. All of the information here is presented with a good heart and to the best of my ability, but research everything thoroughly—and be skeptical of anything that sounds too good to be true. Your choices are up to you.

Chapter Seven

Long-Term Business Growth

There's going to come a time when you are ready for the next step. You have a solid foundation: good credit, experience, connections, drive, and know-how. It's time to pull all your resources together as you start leveraging your situation and developing sources of wealth.

Focus, Not Luck

Some people gaze on the successful person and say, "How lucky they were!" Think again! To be in the top 20 percent of the economic class of our society, you have to make adjustments to your course of life. Rather than hoping for luck, it is important to focus your time and energy on what counts:

- Make connections with like-minded people.

- Use time to your advantage, with both a long investment horizon and good day-to-day practices.

- Be patient. Do the research. Develop and revise your decisions.

- Get out of your comfort zone and be willing to risk (and leverage) what you already have for something bigger.

- Continue to be motivated by reaching for your next goal.

- Be open to possibilities and ready to change direction.

- Enjoy what you do.

One of the best ways to put these goals into practice is to associate with people who have the same goals as you do, even if they're in wildly different fields. It's the mind-set, not the industry, that makes the difference.

Success and Common Goals

One organization that provided me with support, solutions, and colleagues who were as focused as I was on success was the American Education League (AEL). The AEL was a nonprofit group formed to instill American pride. Being part of the AEL was a truly inspirational time in my life. Meetings by the board were monthly and the members were captains of industry. We were joined in our desire to support enterprising young adults in American businesses. These young adults were handpicked from their submission into our yearly essay contests. These contests would encompass current economic topics and the winners would receive monetary awards.

I personally appreciated the learning opportunities that came my way just by surrounding myself with such successful people. While we were united in our core purpose of helping younger people, we also talked to each other about our lives and business concerns. They were all self-starters who, like me, had little to nothing to start with. My first job was shining shoes at the age of five! But in addition to our shared bootstrapped backgrounds, there was also a common mind-set. The members were all entrepreneurs who knew their businesses inside and out, had the courage to take risks, and had developed the resilience to not be easily dejected. This is an overlooked but very important skill set. Things will go wrong! My parents went bankrupt not once, but twice. You have to be prepared to handle the unexpected and, if necessary, start over again.

All the members were confident in their ability to succeed. Many of them invested long hours in their business and did whatever it took to solve the daily problems. No matter what industry we were in, we were all challenged by the same types of problems, such as government regulations, labor disputes, competition, expansion, and debt. Talking these over, hearing other people's successes, mistakes, and suggestions, provided constant opportunities to learn. You need to find a group that does this for you. You need a group such as AEL to draw understanding and encouragement.

Even more importantly, you need people with a common focus on success. Here are some success stories of my fellow AEL members.

Franchise

A good friend of mine decided to sell hot dogs as a street vendor with only a few hundred dollars' investment. He continued adding locations until he was able to start a fast-food restaurant. Not ready to stop there, he added more and more locations all over the West Coast. He gave many people a chance to jump into fast-food franchise restaurants based on his formula. His greatest pride was in how many families he could support by adding more jobs in more locations.

The thing to notice here is that he didn't start out knowing everything there was to know about fast food. He didn't wait until he was an expert to begin. He started small, with a hot dog cart and a few hundred dollars, and he learned the business little by little. He learned which locations were best, which types of food people wanted, how to sell and make people want to come back. He learned about competition, pricing, licensing, inventory, spoilage. He learned things you could only know by being in the trenches, and he learned them with a very small investment. He built his business step by step, growing patiently and waiting for the right moment, the right opportunity, to expand into an actual physical space, which obviously has a lot more risk to it than a cart or truck you can move around. And he was generous with his knowledge, helping others learn the ropes as well. It's important both to grow deliberately, making sure you are ready for the next step, and to be willing to help others and pay forward the help you received on your way up.

Product

Another good friend of mine was an expert machinist. He became proficient by working in a machine shop and developed his abilities and leadership until he made it to foreman level. He was very bothered, however, by his employer's sloppiness and always falling behind the production schedule. In his position, he had no control of the problem. One day, he reached a breaking point and decided to quit working for this guy and start his own machine shop. He found a location, rented equipment, and trained a workforce to do excellent work on time. His company developed a reputation for being an excellent machine shop. He, too, continued to expand, learning the completely different skill set of how to run a business, and became a captain of industry. It all grew out of his own expertise and his passion for excellence.

Dealership

Another friend was a top salesman at an auto dealership. When the company went into bankruptcy, he decided to open his own dealership. He borrowed enough cash to open it, but he used up his starting capital in the first three months. In the fourth month, just in time, his business popped. Why? It all came down to his expertise at advertising and training other salespeople. After one year, he was making a six-figure income. Several years later, he opened up one of the biggest dealerships of its kind at the time.

Marketing is a key aspect of any business. If you have repeat customers and you only need a small customer base, maybe you can rely on word of mouth. But for most businesses, and certainly for something like a car dealership, you need a lot of people who know who you are and why they should trust you to meet their needs. Remember, their needs aren't only a good product; people need to feel safe, that they're not being swindled, that you will take care of any problems that go wrong. Marketing isn't just about building name recognition—it's about building a feeling of trust around that name.

Broker

One friend became a real estate broker after he retired from a government job. Since he knew how to prepare financial statements for investors, he decided to specialize in income property. He would do an analysis of the property and would only take a listing if the seller's price made sense to a buyer. He quickly developed a reputation for competent, clear, no-pressure deals because of his effective, transparent analysis. You knew you'd get a fair price with him as your broker, on both sides of the table.

Think about how you can take your expertise from one area of your life and translate it to a new opportunity or business. You don't have to do things the way everyone else does them if you can think of a better way—and by better, I mean fairer to everyone. Your special skills can improve any business, and you'll enjoy using your expertise in a new way. It also sets you apart and makes you the go-to person for the people looking for what you have to offer.

Real Estate Property Management

Back to my own story. Buying my income properties wasn't the real turning point for me. I was still behaving like an employee. I mowed all the lawns myself. I painted the walls. The whole family got into the act—we all took care of the properties, and we did well financially. I was proud of our work. But I was still thinking like someone who didn't have enough money to hire staff; I still felt I had to do everything myself.

And then I had surgery. My wife, Bernice, laid down the law:

"Robert," she told me, "you can't go out and cut the lawns anymore. I'm going to hire a gardener, whether you like it or not." I suddenly realized that I had the know-how to develop property, but I wasn't doing as much in that area as I could because I was spending my time and energy cutting grass!

When you are in the thick of making things work, it can be difficult to see with any clarity what's really happening. Realigning your focus is so important. Take a new vision, see yourself for what you could be, not what you currently are. It's important to put your energies where they can do the most good. When I stopped cutting grass and started managing property, that's when I leveraged not just my money, but also my expertise. It made all the difference.

One thing about real estate: You can't be afraid to admit when you've made a mistake. It's important for you to be clear-eyed, even about an investment you've already made.

Here's an example from my own life. I once owned a huge apartment building in Los Angeles. It was a tremendous investment and had lots of apartments, but I wasn't actually taking home very much money at all. First, I was swamped with debt on the capital it had required to purchase the building. Second, it was a big building, requiring a lot of upkeep. Third, the neighborhood wasn't improving. I wasn't getting enough tenants or the kind of stable tenants I needed to keep enough money rolling in, and I didn't have a lot of slack because of all the debt I was carrying.

Meanwhile, the guy down the street with a building half the size of mine was walking out with at least twice the money I made every month. He hadn't taken on as much debt as I had and the building didn't require the same investment in upkeep. And while we may have had the same problems with the neighborhood and the timing, he had more resources to face them because, again, he wasn't drowning under massive debt. So on paper, I had far more capital, but what did I have it for? The question you always want to ask yourself is: What is the return on my capital?

I ended up selling the building and took a big hit, but I never regretted getting out. The building I sold for practically nothing thirty years ago is still nearly worthless today. Instead of hanging on, pretending I could make it work, I turned the corner, I learned, and I moved forward. Five years later, I reinvested someplace else and made far more than what I'd lost: I bought a building for $130,000, and it's worth $3 million to $4 million now. But I could only do that because I'd learned from my mistakes.

Take your loss! Forget about your feelings, forget about trying to look good. Move on, learn, and do better next time.

Publishing

I'm a big fan of publishing. So much is achieved with the written word. When I go into a library, I'm like a child going into a candy store. The resources are countless; everything you could ever want to know, you will find in the library. A well-stocked library is the measure of a community.

I wanted to do my part in contributing to this great resource. Years ago, I took over a newspaper as the publisher; eventually, I began publishing books, like the one you're reading, to add to the knowledge in the libraries. In addition, with modern technology and e-books, the cost of producing a book can be profitable and far less risky than having to print a thousand at a time.

Publishing has been a rewarding business to me in more ways than just financial. It has been my pleasure to develop reading material on areas of intense interest to me, such as extraordinary Italians and Italian Americans. Working with writers has been a joy. Writers are creators, starting with a blank page and ultimately delivering information on any topic from joy to sadness, and from our current society to societies of the past.

You, too, can share your story or information that you are passionate about. Whether you are a writer yourself or someone who wants to work with writers to articulate your vision, the advent of e-books has made it possible to get into the publishing game with very little investment.

Mortgages

Here's another story from my own life. When I arrived in California in 1955, the housing market was booming. Contractors were building track houses, and in order to have enough money to keep building, here's how they worked their financing: When the home was sold, the new homeowner obtained a primary mortgage loan of 80 percent, had a down payment of 5 percent, and then the contractor took back a loan of 15 percent. To get the funds to make more developments, the contractor would sell their note for as much as a 50 percent discount to a private lender.

What an opportunity!

Here's what I did: I cashed in the annuity my dad had set up when I was eight years old, and went into being a private lender. Adding to that, while I was still in college, I bought notes at a 50 percent discount. Everyone helped me understand the business. I enjoyed it, but as always, things changed. Banks eventually started lending 95 percent of mortgage loans, which dried up the private lending business.

And then in 2010, another window opened up to be in the business of lending money for real estate loans. This was after loans were made on overvalued homes to unqualified lenders, and in a matter of one year, the real estate market collapsed. Borrowers were "underwater," owing more on their loan than the value of their house. Banks foreclosed on some properties and held back from making new loans. But after the market settled down, this reluctance by banks to lend gave the private lenders, including me, a chance to get back into the market. We made our own valuation of properties and borrowers. A lifetime of working in real estate and an understanding of the business from my earlier foray into private lending set me up for success. We formed a corporation and loan documents were quickly drawn up. A specialist for loan analysis was hired, loan brokers were informed, and we were in business.

The lesson here is that no experience is ever lost, and opportunities are cyclical. You can't go into something thinking it has to be your business forever or it doesn't count; learning every step of the way will allow you to parlay expertise from one industry to another. And you should be on the lookout for opportunities to re-emerge. Timing is everything, but only if you're prepared to take advantage of it.

How to Start Your Own Business

There are basic steps to starting your business. While the details will depend on the type of business, there are some general questions to ask or ideas to consider:

- What credentials do you need? This is apart from the expertise itself. Do you need a specific degree or certificate? What about a license? Acquaint yourself with all the codes and regulations for your business.

- Get some hands-on experience in the arena. Remember my friend with his hot dog cart? What's your version of that? Can you intern somewhere, or work for someone else, like my machinist friend, to learn what you like and don't like about the business and the way other people run their companies? Learn as much as you can about every facet of the industry you are working in.

- Develop relationships. You need prospects or a following of potential clients before you are ready to start your business. You should have about 50 percent of the potential clients you'll need lined up before you announce you're open for business.

- Prepare a budget and have a working capital to carry you for six months. Don't expect to make money at first. You need to be able to stay in business long enough to be successful.

- You need a good support team. Network, get recommendations, and line up staffing possibilities and the professional help, such as accounting and legal affairs, that you will need to kick off your business.

- Find the right location. If people need to visit you in person to make your business work, location, including parking and foot traffic, could be a make-or-break decision.

- Determine the best way to market your business to stand out. Don't know much about marketing? The time to learn is before you open your business, not after you launch. Where can you get some low-stakes experience? Is there a nonprofit you could join to work on their marketing? Where could you meet people who know more than you do and learn from them?

- Don't burn any bridges, don't yell at your boss when you quit, and always, always have multiple backup plans. What's the worst that can happen? Okay, pretend it just happened. What would you do? Set up your safety net now, before you need it.

Niche

It's amazing to see new business developed and how it provides prosperity to the person who could see the future. What didn't exist fifty years ago has become commonplace. I'm not just talking about the phenomenal growth of cell phones, although that's an obvious one. But where once there was tremendous flight from downtown areas to the suburbs, now, all across America, there is a movement back to once-abandoned city properties. We've seen the conversion to swanky apartments by developers who say the potential of these areas has brought enormous growth and solutions for housing demands. The shift from industrial to sedentary jobs brought on a host of needs for exercise; membership gyms, classes, and personal home equipment boomed. Organic farming, local produce, and farm-to-table movements have changed the face of the American farm. Everywhere you look, in every industry, massive changes are in progress. The changes are so rapid that technicians and engineers are having to learn new skills and transition to completely new industries.

What this means for you is that there are many niches, many

opportunities to expand and/or change our way of living. You, too, can look to the future and develop the business of tomorrow.

Business Development

The process of business development is not the same as, say, development for a law or medical career. In both of those areas, you go to school to learn the correct way of doing something. Business education is much more flexible; there may be things that have worked for someone else, but you will almost always have to adapt whatever you've learned to your own industry, new technology, and your own skill set. This can lead to a very diverse career.

And it's open to anyone. Through our country's growth, we became a world leader. Our market economy, limited government control, and a can-do attitude has raised the standard of living for most. Our American spirit has catapulted us into amazing inventions and opportunities. Our economy has produced a strong, vibrant middle class. There is mobility in our classes from poor to middle to rich, and all enjoy services and products beyond our forefathers' dreams. Every single one of us can set our sights on a better life.

Here are some keys:

- **POSITION** yourself in a vibrant career that shows promise. Get the training you need to do well. Embrace excellence.

- Spot a **TREND** that has a future. The metaphor with the advent of the steam engine was "do not try to sell buggy whips." You want to be in an industry that is growing.

- Be **FLEXIBLE** to reevaluate your circumstances. Don't pretend nothing has changed. As I write this, the 2020 coronavirus pandemic is in full swing. When the pandemic hit, people were suddenly working from home and had to learn how to conference online. Pretending you can still network in person during such a time won't help your career grow. While this is an extreme moment in history, things are always changing. Assess your abilities and refocus your energies, shore up your skills, or even change direction if that's what is needed to meet changes in your career path.

- Search **CONNECTIONS** and relationships for resources. The key to success in networking is to be interdependent. Associate with the people who can help you and whom you can help.

- Establish **CREDIT** for sources of funds. Maximize your capital net worth to use for credit. Leverage what you have. Don't miss payments. Your credit score and your reputation are both gold.

Be Relevant

In whatever business you wish to be in, make sure you are all in. This includes being relevant. Do people really need what you offer? Is there justification for your time, energy, and resources to be in a particular business? Don't just jump into something without first checking that there is a need for your product or service or skill set. Proof of concept can keep you from devoting your resources to something that will never pay off.

Cost Benefit

One of the major things you will be doing when you run your own company is cost-benefit analysis. Decisions always have to be made and remade, again and again. One of the worst things you can do is think that you can make a decision and stick with it forever. You may not be able to stick with it beyond the first quarter! Early decisions, in particular, need to be evaluated in the face of reality and on-the-ground experiences. But even once you're established, changes continue because there are always so many moving parts. Ideas change; your staff changes; there are new technologies, new regulations, and sometimes pandemics. Forces beyond our control influence us and our businesses, and it would be foolhardy to pretend otherwise.

To benefit from these changes instead of being undone by them, we must adapt and be flexible. The wrong decision can be costly; sticking to the wrong decision can be disastrous. As we evaluate and choose our direction, we must weigh the cost benefit of each decision. Intuition is a good trait—it allows you to see possibility—but without analysis, you shouldn't make a decision. I'm a fan of slow and steady, small stakes at first, learning and testing along the way. Analyze everything. Choices have consequences. And remember that making business decisions for personal reasons will likely keep you from success. Who cares what someone else is doing or what your cousin thinks of you? Trying to look good or smart or successful is no replacement for actually being honest, thorough, and committed to working hard.

Evaluate the numbers. Every cost you have must benefit your company in a real way. Projected outcomes may or may not happen; this is why you have a backup plan. Being willing to reevaluate means being willing to have been wrong, and that honesty with yourself can save your business from spiraling when the unexpected happens. And it will.

Losing Ideas

It doesn't always work out when you see a possibility to create a business. I've had a couple of missteps, and in the interest of transparency (and you learning from my mistakes), I will share them with you.

The Moving Business

I'm in real estate and, in particular, rental properties. At one point, I observed that there appeared to be a need for another moving and storage company in our area. In our time of flux, people move in and out of rental apartments often, and could use a moving company that also had a storage facility as a component. Seemed like a great idea! However, after studying the licensing requirements of transferring people's stuff from one place to another, not to mention keeping it at one location—plus the labor, the cost of moving trucks, and the vast quantities of insurance we would need—it was hard to see a profitable business. I did my cost-benefit analysis and I let the idea go.

Housekeeping Service

With all the adults in a household working full-time (a cultural shift that has developed in my lifetime), it seemed there was a need for a cleaning service. For it to be profitable, it had to work automatically, almost like in a hotel. But everyone's needs were different. A lot of people didn't want strangers in their house when no one else was home, even to clean the place. And the housekeepers we looked to hire required supervision by someone who could speak the housekeeper's native language. There were also marketing issues; how could we get the word out and stand out from other services? In the end, there were simply too many moving parts for me to see a way to make it work for us.

Six Degrees of Connectivity

Connections are critical to your success, and because of that, it's important to understand the Six Degrees of Connectivity. Whether you are starting a business or are already established, you will go farther faster using your Six Degrees. What this means is that, starting with everyone you know, you can grow your acquaintance list (and potential prospect list) by connecting through them to the people they know. Your list could start with family, friends, and neighbors and be added to with acquaintances at school, church, and clubs. Here's the important bit: You need to tell your connections about your business and ask them to tell other people. If you tell six people and each of those tells six more people, the word of mouth about your business could quickly grow to as many as 46,656 people who have now heard of you. Don't believe me? Take a look at any social media platform. A post that goes viral follows this kind of pattern. Even if you're not on social media, you can harness the power of your connections by having a clear value and a memorable offer. Give them a reason to share your information, and you can exponentially expand the number of people who know of you and your service or product.

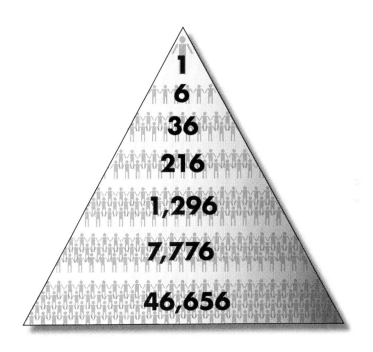

Think Like an Executive

The preparation for the working world that you got in high school, vo-tech, or college was a bird's-eye view. The biggest step you can take on the path to wealth is to move from employee to supervisor, manager, and someday president of whatever industry you're in. The pathway to this is training. Limited training may curtail your upward mobility; higher positions depend on your own growth, both in industry-specific skills and in leadership. In order to go from the mailroom to the executive desk, you will need to constantly be learning. Formal education is good, but nothing beats on-the-ground learning from those around you.

You have to immerse yourself in various facets of a company's activities. Be sure to challenge yourself and not stay stagnant in your current position. Your eye should also be on ways to increase the value of the company. You should constantly be looking for better ways to do your job or to set things up for other people's success. The administration may not take your suggestions, but when you're ready to step into leadership—either there, for a different company, or for your own business—you will have a deep understanding of best practices and innovative solutions because you'll always be looking for a better way.

I'm a big believer in getting advice from people you respect, but at some point you have to make your own decisions and learn to trust your judgment. If you are forever going to the group to ask for your next move, you are insecure. You will second-guess yourself and blame others, and it will slow you down. A dependence on group-think weakens your leadership.

It reminds me of the story about a man who wanted to design the perfect horse. After going to the committee, taking everyone's needs and ideas into account, he had a design made by group-think. The problem was the design ended up looking like a camel.

An inventor cannot invent in a group. A good leader knows when to lean on their team for support, delegates tasks or research to others, and allows team members to take responsibility and grow themselves. But ultimately, the buck stops with you. A leader needs clarity for his or her own vision.

Chapter Eight

How Money Works

Money is the lubricant for everything we do. In just about every transaction, money comes into play. It is a resource that continually changes, but the trick is to see it as a renewable resource. You are not a dragon hoarding a pile of gold. You want to use your money, leveraging it (and, whenever possible, leveraging other people's money as well) to create new opportunities for it to grow.

Supply and Demand

The cost of virtually anything is governed by supply and demand. That means how much of a thing is available and how much demand is there for it. My college professor used to say, "Think of sand on a beach. There is a lot of it, but how many people want to buy it?"

This is true for investment as well, to determine the rate of return. Say there's a resource—gold, for instance—and the demand goes up while the supply goes down, then the cost of that resource will increase. Conversely, a company's value can rise or fall depending on its access to a resource. For example, if a coal company finds another mountain of coal, its stock will go up because of the increase in the available supply. If the company relies on a coal mining operation that is depleting, its stock prices will go down. The value of the company is dependent upon its ability to harness that natural resource; fewer resources mean the company is worth less as a whole.

Product prices have many cycles. A fad can produce a great demand, causing an upswing in cost; if the fad fades away, the price goes down. You'll see this a lot with some ridiculous things—I remember one year when Tickle Me Elmo dolls were going for crazy prices at Christmastime—but it can be true of almost anything, including clothes, diet, or sports activities, and all of those can have market ramifications. If technology requires a new resource, such as lithium, the value of that resource can skyrocket. Lead is potentially hazardous; it used to be added to everything from paint to gasoline, but since the risks became known, it has been used much less, so down went the price of lead. Stock prices can be influenced by government regulation; for instance, the Affordable Care Act changed the way the medical industry operates. Sometimes a new technology, like cell phones, will forever change our lives. Some movements can be a swift up or down, and at other times it can take years for a movement to become obvious.

When you're evaluating something as an investment, you are always to some extent gambling on its value increasing, on the demand for it outstripping the supply. You can rely on common sense and research, but this can be a roller coaster. There are so many factors to take into account, and many things are beyond your control. I'll just say this: Don't gamble what you can't afford to lose, and stay away from consumer fads unless you're prepared to get in and get out very quickly. You couldn't give away a Tickle Me Elmo once that year's presents were opened.

Devaluation of Purchasing Power

Devaluation of purchasing power is a critical concept to understand wealth. Here's the gist of it: What a dollar will buy in the future is not what a dollar buys now. Your dollar today will inevitably buy less in the years ahead as prices go up. In 1920, a pound of coffee cost $0.47.

Today, one hundred years later, it costs about $15/pound, an increase of 3,200 percent. But you don't need me to tell you that prices go up. If you've been shopping for any length of time, I'm sure you've already noticed how much more you spend on the same items at the grocery store or the gas pump. The key is to recognize that this will continue, and that a dollar today will buy much less in the future.

Inflation

Here's what happens: More dollars are printed by the government to buy more goods and to use more money to pay off debt. This is called inflation. The chart below shows the projected rate of inflation based on a 2.5 percent increase per year which is conservative.

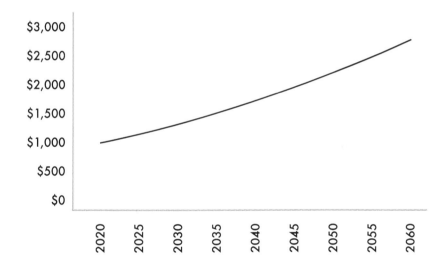

This is both bad news and good news. The bad news is you're going to need more money than you think you will in retirement. As you can see from the above chart, in 2060 it will cost you $2,685 to buy the equivalent of $1,000 in 2020. Inflation can cause a serious hit by the time you retire.

The good news is, as time goes on, you are paying down long-term debt, such as a mortgage, in cheaper and cheaper dollars. As with everything, inflation can work in your favor or it can work against you.

The trick is to understand the difference and leverage it as much as you can to your own advantage.

SIMPLE INTEREST

ORIGINAL $1,000 EARNING 6% PER YEAR

YEAR	BEGINNING BALANCE	INTEREST EARNED	ENDING BALANCE
2020	$1,000	$60	$1,060
2025	$1,000	$60	$1,300
2030	$1,000	$60	$1,600
2035	$1,000	$60	$1,900
2040	$1,000	$60	$2,200
2045	$1,000	$60	$2,500
2050	$1,000	$60	$2,800
2055	$1,000	$60	$3,100
2060	$1,000	$60	$3,400

COMPOUND INTEREST

ORIGINAL $1,000 EARNING 6% ON THE NEW BALANCE

YEAR	BEGINNING BALANCE	INTEREST EARNED	ENDING BALANCE
2020	$1,000	$60	$1,060
2025	$1,060	$278	$1,338
2030	$1,338	$453	$1,791
2035	$1,791	$606	$2,397
2040	$2,397	$811	$3,208
2045	$3,207	$1,084	$4,292
2050	$4,292	$1,452	$5,744
2055	$5,743	$1,943	$7,687
2060	$7,686	$2,600	$10,287

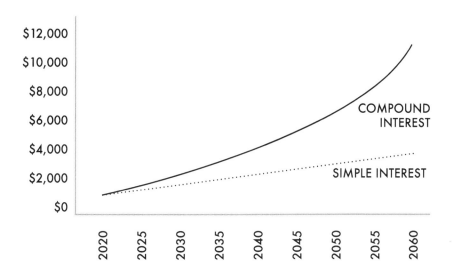

Interest

You probably already have a savings account with a bank or credit union that, very likely, gives you a small amount of monthly interest. As I write this, interest rates remain low, so you're probably unimpressed with how much interest your money is earning in a regular savings account. But it wasn't always like that, and rates won't always be this low. So let me explain some concepts.

Simple vs. Compound Interest

Simple interest is calculated at a fixed rate on the same balance of the original savings or investment. So each year, you earn the same amount of interest, even though your balance increases. The interest only accrues on your original investment.

With compound interest, however, the interest earned is added to the original investment, so the next computation is made on both the original deposit *and* the previous interest. In effect, interest is earned on the interest—this is what's known as compounding.

As you can see from the chart, at the end of forty years, your balance with a simple interest account is $3,400 (from the original $1,000 investment), whereas from that same investment, your balance in the compound interest account is $10,287—more than twice as much. That is the beauty of compound interest.

In other words, with compound interest, you end up with more than double the money you would have with a simple interest account.

Rule of 72

The Rule of 72 gives you a sense of how long it will take to double your money. The formula is: Divide the rule number (72) by the annual interest rate (R) to find out the approximate time (T) required for doubling (72 ÷ R = T).

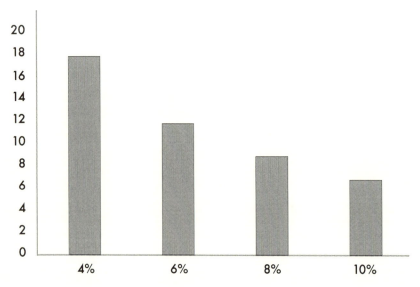

YEARS REQUIRED TO DOUBLE YOUR MONEY

A rise or fall in the interest rate can make a big difference in the outcome. To go from a 4 percent return to a 6 percent return means your money will double in twelve years instead of eighteen years. The higher the interest rate, the more dramatic the difference.

It's important to look at your options and see where your money can earn the best rate. Sometimes that comes with some risk, but other times, it can be the difference between keeping the money sitting in your savings account versus earning more in something like a better bond or a dividend on stock—a very safe investment, but one that offers a higher interest rate in exchange for restrictions placed on your ability to withdraw funds for a certain length of time.

Cycles

Timing is everything. There is a time to buy and a time to sell—or at least not buy. The problem is we can never be certain exactly what time we're in. There is no crystal ball; we may expect an upward trend to continue or a downward trend to break, but there's no certainty.

The important thing to understand is that while we can't (and shouldn't try) to time the market (I'll talk about one technique, dollar cost averaging, in a little bit), there are some indicators to pay attention to. Markets will reliably respond to multiple factors:

DOWN MARKET

› Are we at war? The stock market tends to go down when we are at war and go up after a war is over.

› Are we in a recession or depression? That tends to push the market down.

› Unemployment or a nervous consumer base could result in a drop in sales, which would push the market down.

UP MARKET

> A new technology or discovery could push a market up.

> Full employment could mean more production and greater sales, pushing the market up.

> Quality of life makes the market go up. People do more, live longer, are more productive. Everything that goes with the good life can push the market up.

Investment Movement

Stocks go up. Stocks go down. While the market as a whole may go one way, individual investments might outpace it or even go in the opposite direction. The highest upward movement in your investment portfolio may seem amazing, while the investment that barely moves the needle may seem the safest. Neither is necessarily so.

There have been periods when housing sold for 50 percent of what it cost for it to be built. There was also a time when a corporate stock dropped 50 percent. When markets fall, that's generally a good time to buy—assuming you understand that the drop won't last, and you have the cash to buy. Never get so panicked that you sell low. Markets go down, and then they go back up. There's opportunity to buy low when they're down and to sell high when they're up. Panic leads to terrible decision making, so the most important thing you can do is to understand that markets are always in flux and make your plans accordingly.

Stocks move for a variety of reasons, including reasons that have nothing to do with the value of the company itself. If the whole market goes down, that has an impact even on companies whose value is solid. Sometimes there are problems within a single company that are reflected in its stock price, while other times there are problems in the entire industry. But whether the movement is easy to explain—a corporate scandal can send prices tumbling, while a promising new drug can send them soaring—or impossible to fathom, the bottom-line concern is to be objective and use the direction of the movement to make your decisions on whether you buy or sell.

Price/Earnings Ratio

What is the price/earnings ratio of a stock? In other words, what's the price of a share of the company's stock compared to the company's earnings per share? If it's low, the stock may be considered under-valued, and so stock share prices tend to go up, while if the rate reached a traditional high, the stock could be peaking and have nowhere to go but down. If a lot of stocks, or important stocks, are overvalued and heading down, that could bring the entire market down with them.

In the long run, the biggest profits come from buying low and selling high. This is easier said than done. What is more predictable is to be involved and active. If you don't participate, you can't expect to win.

As an investor, you can't have an allegiance to past decisions. I was buying stock in companies that produced products I used. It felt good to support the company and I believed in the product, yet when the stock reached what I considered to be its peak, I sold. I alone could not buy enough to stop the stock from ever going down—just as I couldn't sell enough to keep it from going up. You have to decide what you believe the potential of that company is, pay attention to things that may impact its performance, and be willing to sell when it's high.

Let me repeat that: You do have to sell at some point, and ideally when the stock is worth a lot more than you paid for it. You don't have to sell at the perfect moment, when it's as high as it will ever be, because you have no control over when that moment will happen. As I said, there is no crystal ball. You sell when you think the time is right, and then you have to be okay with your decision. It's easy to feel good about selling when the stock goes down afterward, but remember that even if the stock keeps going up, if you sold it for more than you paid for it, you made money. That's the idea; you did well! And ideally, you will be moving your profits into something else that will also make you money—different stocks, a new business, real estate. People go nuts trying to time the market. Make your decision, learn from it, and move on.

Another thing to be wary of is percentages. Ten percent of a cheap stock is not a lot of money; 10 percent of a large amount is quite a bit more. For instance, if a stock goes up 20 percent, and then down 20 percent, it's not back to its original amount. That second 20 percent is of a larger number, and so it's more; you've actually lost a little money.

So don't let percentages sway you too much. Remember the underlying number is more important. A $100 investment that goes up 50 percent isn't worth more than a $1,000 investment that goes up 5 percent; in fact, your profit is the same ($50).

People think you have to make split-second decisions. Don't you believe it. It may be better to move slower than faster so that you're making decisions based on solid reasoning—you're acting, not simply reacting. Shifts in the market from day-to-day events could just be temporary. Stay with the trend of what your stock is doing. If you bought a stock at $100 that went up to $120, only to go down to $110, keep in mind that you haven't had a loss. Your initial investment was $100, not $120; you (and the stock) are still up. Keeping your head when others panic is a great way to make money in the stock market.

This is a good time for me to again make the disclaimer that I'm not going to give you specific market advice. What I want you to see are the options you have, and ways to mitigate your risk. No investment, not even purchasing your own home, is entirely risk-free.

But if you want to invest in stocks, historically, the market has risen over long periods of time and an index fund allows you to grow your investment with it. Index funds and mutual funds are simply funds whose holdings mirror that of a market index, like the Dow Jones Industrial Average. (I'll be talking more about index funds and giving examples later on.)

- If you don't want to invest in a fund, but would rather purchase an individual stock, dollar cost averaging allows you to buy more when it's low and buy less (but still some) when it's high, averaging out your risk.

- Investing in an IRA (individual retirement account) can provide tax advantages and keep you from touching the principal, allowing your nest egg to grow.
- Investing in your children's education can put them in a position where they will be financially stable as adults.

You want to diversify your investments not just in terms of the stock market, but also in terms of your life. Your portfolio should reflect your values and goals and encompass a broad range of investment types.

Let's talk about these ideas in the next chapter.

Chapter Nine

Smart Investing

Now let's take a detailed look at the investment options I mentioned at the end of the last chapter, including dollar cost averaging, individual retirement accounts, college savings programs, and more.

Dollar Cost Averaging

When I was transferred to North Carolina from New York, I was really on my own. It was then, at the age of twenty-one, that I came across a stockbroker who advised me to use a part of my paycheck to buy stock in the Canadian Railroad. Each week, I took his advice. In three years, in spite of the stock fluctuations, I had overall growth. I made money. You can, too. The magic is dollar cost averaging.

Here's why it works: By spending a set amount of money on stocks at regular intervals, you are in no way attempting to "beat the market." There's no guesswork involved, no luck, no skill. Let's say you set up an automatic purchase of $100 every month. When the market is up, that $100 will buy fewer shares of stock, but each is worth a little more. When the market is down, $100 will buy more shares, but they're each worth a little less. Over time, the market rises. So does the value of your investment.

This weekly routine of dollar cost averaging, catching the up and down movement, can be very successful over a long period of time. Time is your friend here. This is not day trading. This is not where you get to be exciting and gamble on what will and won't go up. It's not trying to time the market, and it certainly isn't selling when the bottom falls out. On the contrary, that's a great time to buy because you get more shares for your money!

Dollar cost averaging is a boring way to wealth and—let me stress this—BORING IS GOOD. It's reliable. Pick a strong stock that isn't going anywhere, or pick a mutual fund that mirrors the averages, and be consistent. (Quick definition here: A mutual fund is essentially a portfolio of diversified holdings that shareholders own together. A share in a mutual fund represents a percentage of the entire portfolio, rather than one single stock. Mutual fund fees pay for the professional management of the fund.)

However you choose to invest, the key to accumulating wealth is to stay the course, because sooner or later with an optimistic attitude your investment will grow along with the economy.

Investing for Retirement

Let's talk about retirement. Social security will never provide a decent standard of living, nor was it meant to. I know, you're young, you may have barely started your career, and already I want you to think about retiring? You bet I do. Because the sooner you start thinking about it, the more time you have to build that retirement fund—and the less likely you are to outlive your money.

The first step you need to take is, happily, one you can take immediately, today. You can start paying yourself first.

Here's what that means: Every paycheck, you set aside an amount of money that goes directly into a savings account—ideally, one that is hard for you to touch. As I've already mentioned, I'm a big believer in socking money away into a savings account that you can use down the road for starting a business or buying property. But in addition to what we'll call your finance fund and, of course, your emergency savings, you need to put regular deposits into a third savings program, one you can't touch until you're ready to retire.

This is where starting early makes the most difference, because this money will grow over the longest period of time. Also, remember that dollar cost averaging I was talking about? This is where it really comes in handy. If, every paycheck, some money is automatically put into something as simple as an IRA index fund, you won't even notice it's gone. It will buy more shares of the fund when stocks are down and fewer shares when stocks are up, but the overall value will climb as the market does. You are legally allowed to put a certain amount in every year once you start earning a paycheck, and you should max that out every year. Don't make the mistake of thinking you'll put more in when your income goes up—that's a trap. First of all, you won't; your standard of living will increase right along with your income and you'll never want to start, so you might as well bite the bullet and start today. And second, investing now gives more time for that money to grow, which is the key to building your retirement nest egg. Do not deprive yourself of critical years by starting late. (Although if you haven't started and you're already mid-career, don't take that to mean it's not worth starting to save now. It is. Start today, no matter where you are.)

There are two types of IRAs (individual retirement accounts): traditional and Roth. The big difference is that with a traditional IRA, the money goes in tax-free (that is, you can deduct your contributions from your gross earnings before taxable income), but the money is taxed when you take it out. With a Roth IRA, it's the opposite: no tax benefit today, but since the money has already been taxed, you don't have to pay tax on it again when you take it out. This is a bit simplified and you should thoroughly look into any IRA plan you are considering—both plans have detailed regulations and should be compared. Also, different firms offer different options for your IRA funds; it's definitely not one-size-fits-all.

Roth IRA

The Roth provision was set up by Congress to encourage people to save for their future. It used to be that employers provided for their staff's retirement, but we no longer live in a world where that is the case—or where you would even consider working for one firm for your entire career. The Roth was meant to be an alternative, allowing people to essentially set up their own retirement plans. Contributions to the plan are made after taxes have been paid, so there are no taxes when you draw from the fund. All growth in the fund is not taxed, which can be a tremendous boon when it comes time to withdraw the money.

Traditional IRA

Your traditional IRA contribution is made yearly with tax-free funds. The tax is paid when you retire and withdraw the money. The reason you might want to do it this way is that, presumably, your income after retirement will be lower than it is now, and so you'll be in a lower tax bracket. This is not always true, but it's not a bad assumption for many people. Also, some people benefit from the annual tax deduction; just be sure to know what you're doing (or hire an accountant or tax preparer who knows the law) because there are limits to the amount you can deduct if, for instance, you or your spouse is covered by a retirement plan at work and your income exceeds certain levels. Also, Congress changes the rules every so often, so you'll need to be aware of what they are.

Again, nothing in this book is meant to serve as legal advice, particularly on tax matters.

Roth vs. Traditional IRA

Now that you have a sense of what the options are, let me show you what they can do for you. The study on the following pages shows the effect of each option, both Roth and traditional IRA, and how the money grows. In the tables, I used a conservative 6 percent compound study—that means that I've assumed your money will grow by 6 percent a year, which is on the low end. Some years, the market does worse, of course, but some years it does much better. The thing to remember is when you're taking a long and diversified (through an index fund, for instance) view of the market, you don't need to worry about recessions along the way. You just keep dollar cost averaging every month and forget about it.

The tables on the following pages demonstrate how your investment can grow. Most people don't miss the money they pay themselves—provided it comes out automatically. Trust me when I say you won't want to rely on willpower to write yourself a check every month for your retirement fund. But paying yourself is the key to the kingdom; this kind of self-rewarding locks in your future. And as you climb into greater income, you can start building other ways to supplement your retirement.

Finally, remember the traditional IRA grows larger because the deduction was made before your adjusted income. There were no taxes paid. The taxes are paid after the distribution from the IRA. On the other hand, in a Roth IRA, the taxes are paid on the current, adjusted gross income, but not on the future withdrawal because that is tax-free.

Page 96 shows two different retirement accounts (with one assuming 20 percent taxes upon distribution) as they are depleted with a yearly $50,000 distribution. The balance continues to earn 6 percent interest compounding every year.

It will take over ten years of withdrawal for the retirement funds to be exhausted. It would appear the funds are equalized. However, the advantage of a traditional IRA is that each year, the beginning balance is always higher (so before you pay down your estate, it is greater, and if you decease before the ten years, your estate has a greater amount). In the Roth case, though, the annual withdraw is tax free, whereas in the traditional IRA, taxes are due upon annual withdraw. But the traditional IRA always has a higher ending balance each year. You start with more money invested and it continues to compound over time.

ROTH IRA

YEAR	GROSS CONTRIB.	25% TAXES	NET CONTRIB.	6% COMPOUND INTEREST	YEAR-END VALUE
1	$6,000	-$1,500	$4,500	$270	$4,770
2	$6,000	-$1,500	$4,500	$556	$9,826
3	$6,000	-$1,500	$4,500	$860	$15,186
4	$6,000	-$1,500	$4,500	$1,181	$20,867
5	$6,000	-$1,500	$4,500	$1,522	$26,889
6	$6,000	-$1,500	$4,500	$1,883	$33,272
7	$6,000	-$1,500	$4,500	$2,266	$40,039
8	$6,000	-$1,500	$4,500	$2,672	$47,211
9	$6,000	-$1,500	$4,500	$3,103	$54,814
10	$6,000	-$1,500	$4,500	$3,559	$62,872
11	$6,000	-$1,500	$4,500	$4,042	$71,415
12	$6,000	-$1,500	$4,500	$4,555	$80,470
13	$6,000	-$1,500	$4,500	$5,098	$90,068
14	$6,000	-$1,500	$4,500	$5,674	$100,242
15	$6,000	-$1,500	$4,500	$6,285	$111,026
16	$6,000	-$1,500	$4,500	$6,932	$122,458
17	$6,000	-$1,500	$4,500	$7,617	$134,575
18	$6,000	-$1,500	$4,500	$8,345	$147,420
19	$6,000	-$1,500	$4,500	$9,115	$161,035
20	$6,000	-$1,500	$4,500	$9,932	$175,467
21	$6,000	-$1,500	$4,500	$10,798	$190,765
22	$6,000	-$1,500	$4,500	$11,716	$206,981
23	$6,000	-$1,500	$4,500	$12,689	$224,170
24	$6,000	-$1,500	$4,500	$13,720	$242,390
25	$6,000	-$1,500	$4,500	$14,813	$261,704
26	$6,000	-$1,500	$4,500	$15,972	$282,176
27	$6,000	-$1,500	$4,500	$17,201	$303,877
28	$6,000	-$1,500	$4,500	$18,503	$326,879
29	$6,000	-$1,500	$4,500	$19,883	$351,262
30	$6,000	-$1,500	$4,500	$21,346	$377,108
TOTAL	$180,000	-$45,000	$135,000	$242,108	$377,108

BUILDING WEALTH 101

TRADITIONAL IRA

YEAR	GROSS CONTRIB.	6% COMPOUND INTEREST	YEAR-END VALUE
1	$6,000	$360	$6,360
2	$6,000	$742	$13,102
3	$6,000	$1,146	$20,248
4	$6,000	$1,575	$27,823
5	$6,000	$2,029	$35,852
6	$6,000	$2,511	$44,363
7	$6,000	$3,022	$53,385
8	$6,000	$3,563	$62,948
9	$6,000	$4,137	$73,085
10	$6,000	$4,745	$83,830
11	$6,000	$5,390	$95,220
12	$6,000	$6,073	$107,293
13	$6,000	$6,798	$120,090
14	$6,000	$7,565	$133,656
15	$6,000	$8,379	$148,035
16	$6,000	$9,242	$163,277
17	$6,000	$10,157	$179,434
18	$6,000	$11,126	$196,560
19	$6,000	$12,154	$214,714
20	$6,000	$13,243	$233,956
21	$6,000	$14,397	$254,354
22	$6,000	$15,621	$275,975
23	$6,000	$16,918	$298,893
24	$6,000	$18,294	$323,187
25	$6,000	$19,751	$348,938
26	$6,000	$21,296	$376,235
27	$6,000	$22,934	$405,169
28	$6,000	$24,670	$435,839
29	$6,000	$26,510	$468,349
30	$6,000	$28,461	$502,810
TOTAL	**$180,000**	**$322,810**	**$502,810**

ROTH IRA DISTRIBUTION AT RETIREMENT

YEAR	VALUE	YEARLY DISTRIB.	TAXES	BALANCE	6% COMPOUND INTEREST	YEAR-END VALUE
1	$377,108	$50,000	$0	$327,108	$19,626	$346,734
2	$346,734	$50,000	$0	$296,734	$17,804	$314,538
3	$314,538	$50,000	$0	$264,538	$15,872	$280,410
4	$280,410	$50,000	$0	$230,410	$13,825	$244,235
5	$244,235	$50,000	$0	$194,235	$11,654	$205,889
6	$205,889	$50,000	$0	$155,889	$9,353	$165,242
7	$165,242	$50,000	$0	$115,242	$6,915	$122,157
8	$122,157	$50,000	$0	$72,157	$4,329	$76,486
9	$76,486	$50,000	$0	$26,486	$1,589	$28,076
10	$28,076	$28,076	$0			

TRADITIONAL IRA DISTRIBUTION AT RETIREMENT

YEAR	VALUE	YEARLY DISTRIB.	20% TAXES	BALANCE	6% COMPOUND INTEREST	YEAR-END VALUE
1	$502,810	$62,500	$12,500	$440,310	$26,419	$466,729
2	$466,729	$62,500	$12,500	$404,229	$24,254	$428,482
3	$428,482	$62,500	$12,500	$365,982	$21,959	$387,941
4	$387,941	$62,500	$12,500	$325,441	$19,526	$344,968
5	$344,968	$62,500	$12,500	$282,468	$16,948	$299,416
6	$299,416	$62,500	$12,500	$236,916	$14,215	$251,131
7	$251,131	$62,500	$12,500	$188,631	$11,318	$199,949
8	$199,949	$62,500	$12,500	$137,449	$8,247	$145,696
9	$145,696	$62,500	$12,500	$83,196	$4,992	$88,187
10	$88,187	$62,500	$12,500	$25,687	$1,541	$27,228
11	$27,228	$27,228	$5,446			

Employer-Sponsored Plans

There are two primary types of employer-sponsored plans to help you save for retirement. The first is what you would think of as a traditional pension plan, which is actually called a **defined benefit plan**. It depends on the number of years you've worked for the company, your position, and possibly a host of other things—including whether or not there's an economic downturn during your retirement. This was the pension plan your grandfather would have had, and while it was once the cornerstone of the retirement world, the 1960s saw many of them implode. Although some safeguards have since been put in place, traditional pension plans have, to a large extent, fallen out of favor. If that's what your employer offers, of course you should take advantage of it, just don't plan to rely on it exclusively for your retirement needs.

The other employer-sponsored plan, which started to take off in the 1990s, is the **defined contribution plan**, typically a 401(k), or if you work for a nonprofit, a 403(b). This plan is similar to your IRA in that you put a set amount of money into a fund account every month and you can access the money on retirement. Here's the big difference: Your employer will typically match a portion of your contribution, up to a certain amount. Let me repeat this, because I want you to understand it: In an employer-matching program, when you put in money, so does your employer—money over and above your salary. It is usually a percentage of your contribution up to a certain limit.

All of this depends on your specific employer's plan, and some employers don't match contributions at all. So talk to your Human Resources department about it right now, because when there is a matching benefit, that is the equivalent of free money. And that free bonus will compound along with your own contribution as the value of the fund grows. Seriously, employer-matching 401(k) programs are a no-brainer.

As always, you should read the fine print, but generally speaking, you should contribute automatically, every paycheck, at least as much as your employer will match. Get the immediate return on investment from your employer's matching funds right off the bat. After that, it's up to you if you want to invest more, if you decide that's the best place for your money. But don't leave matching funds on the table.

People have done some research and found there's one big stumbling block that can keep you from taking advantage of these programs, so I'm going to warn you about it right now: When you go to set up your 401(k) or 403(b), you usually have to pick from a number of mutual funds which one(s) you want to invest in. Sometimes, there are too many choices; scientists have found that when we are overwhelmed with choice, we will shut down and choose nothing, and sure enough, that's often what happens with people faced with too many options for investing. You will find advice saying you should check the fees, you should take into account your investing horizon (which is a fancy way of saying how long you have until you retire), and a whole bunch of other things.

I am here to tell you the only thing you can do wrong is to not pick anything.

As long as your employer is matching your contribution, you are going to come out ahead of the game no matter what you pick, so don't over-worry about the fees. Index funds typically have low fees. Target-date funds do the thinking for you. A target-date fund changes your investment strategy over time. It starts you off with investments that are a little riskier but have potentially higher rewards, and then gets more conservative the closer you are to retirement, when you'll want to conserve capital. You can diversify (always a good idea) by splitting your contribution between two or three funds. If you find yourself starting to get a little crazy, just pick a couple at random and start there. Really, anything is better than not participating—you lose too much by not playing at all. You can always revisit once you've had time to dig in and do the research. Check with your HR department to see how and when you can change your investments. But be making money while you're getting savvy. Don't wait until you have exactly the right answer, because that is the only wrong decision here.

College Savings Plan

There is so much to save for—your emergency fund; your retirement; money that allows you to finance bigger projects or take advantage of opportunities like buying property or starting a business. I bet you can't believe I'm going to tell you to save for something else as well. But of course I am. I'm going to make sure you start saving for your children's future.

Over the last decade or more, college has become very expensive, even in state-run institutions. You might ask yourself, is it worth it? The answer is absolutely, yes. Today, a college degree is the baseline required for a multitude of well-paying jobs. Yes, we need plumbers and electricians, who might need trade school over college, but trade school is not cheap, either. Also, increasingly, those plumbers and electricians might one day want to hang their own shingle. They're going to need enough math and business savvy to keep the books, enough English to be able to market their business and write up brochures, and enough smart, talented, educated friends to help them fill the gaps in their own know-how. A college education gives you knowledge, skills, an ability to do research, and a cohort of people with whom you can start building your professional network. And if you want to be in a white-collar profession, a college degree is nonnegotiable.

You want that for yourself, and you definitely want that for your kids.

In 1996, a college plan was adopted to help families provide a savings account for college education. This was particularly important because tuition and housing became a challenge for many families. The financial inducement was that the accumulation was tax-deferred. Any earnings on this account would not be considered taxable income. The savings account became known as a 529 savings plan. The advantages are summarized below:

- Tax deferred accumulation

- Tax-free earning

- Reduction of estate tax

- Accelerated gift tax investment

COLLEGE SAVINGS PLAN

YEAR	VALUE	YEARLY CONTRIB.	6% COMPOUND INTEREST	YEAR-END VALUE
1		$2,000	$120	$2,120
2	$2,120	$2,000	$247	$4,367
3	$4,367	$2,000	$382	$6,749
4	$6,749	$2,000	$525	$9,274
5	$9,274	$2,000	$676	$11,951
6	$11,951	$2,000	$837	$14,788
7	$14,788	$2,000	$1,007	$17,795
8	$17,795	$2,000	$1,188	$20,983
9	$20,983	$2,000	$1,379	$24,362
10	$24,362	$2,000	$1,582	$27,943
11	$27,943	$2,000	$1,797	$31,740
12	$31,740	$2,000	$2,024	$35,764
13	$35,764	$2,000	$2,266	$40,030
14	$40,030	$2,000	$2,522	$44,552
15	$44,552	$2,000	$2,793	$49,345
16	$49,345	$2,000	$3,081	$54,426
17	$54,426	$2,000	$3,386	$59,811
18	$59,811	$2,000	$3,709	$65,520
19	$65,520	$2,000	$4,051	$71,571
20	$71,571	$2,000	$4,414	$77,985
TOTAL		**$40,000**	**$37,985**	**$77,985**

As with retirement savings, the key is to start early—as early as the day your child is born, so over twenty years you can earn enough to send your child to college. By depositing $2,000 per year compounding at 6 percent, your investment will come to $77,985 on what was a $40,000 investment over twenty years. This is close to four years of state college tuition for one student. Of course, if you have more children, you'll have to save more—and with a 529 savings plan, you can. In fact, other people, such as grandparents, aunts, and uncles, can put money into your child's 529 plan as well. It is a tremendous savings opportunity, and once again, taking advantage of it early and with an automatic deduction from your paycheck is the way to go.

I want to make a quick plug for not discounting top colleges, assuming your child is academically inclined. Universities like Yale, Harvard, and—jumping on the bandwagon as I write this—the University of Southern California have all recently put in place programs offering full tuition to children in families making under a certain amount of income, and a sliding scale for many more. The income levels are between $80,000 and $120,000 per year, so many families who would never have been able to afford private college tuition may now find it less expensive than state schools. Don't assume something is out of your reach. There are often many creative options, and you won't know until you've tried.

Tuition payment options:

- Your own savings

- Government aid
  - Federal aid (FAFSA)
  - State aid
  - Subsidized loans: available for students who have demonstrated financial need
  - Unsubsidized loans: available to students regardless of financial need; students are responsible for repaying interest during all periods.

- Institutional aid, where individual colleges and universities provide funds to their own students

- Private aid
  › Typically, corporations and religious, cultural, professional, and service organizations
  › Private loans
  › Scholarships

- Grants
  › Pell grant: usually awarded to undergraduate students who have not earned a bachelor's degree or professional degree
  › Federal Supplemental Educational Opportunity Grant (FSEOG): for undergraduate students with exceptional financial need
  › Teacher Education Assistance for College and Higher Education (TEACH) grant: for students who are completing or plan to complete coursework for a career in teaching

- Work-study: a work program where the student can earn money that helps them pay for tuition

The important thing to remember is that you will use multiple sources to fund college. While you don't have to rely on only your savings, it's important that you do have them to fall back on. The last thing you want is for your child to be forced to drop out because of lack of finances; it can stall their career in a way that takes years to recover from.

I've spent a lot of time talking about saving for college in terms of your kids, and you may not even have kids of your own yet. I'm hitting it hard because, once again, it's one of those investment opportunities where time is on your side, but only if you start early. Plus, helping your children get the education they need to become self-supporting, contributing members of society is an investment in your own future, and in our future as a society, so for all of those reasons, I want you to get cracking on it. But let's stay with education for a minute longer, and let's talk about you.

You should plan to continue to invest in your education even after you've secured your own college degree. It's not just that technology changes almost as fast as we can keep up, although that's certainly true. It's that developing a practice of lifelong learning will serve you in a way that is priceless.

No matter what business you're in, there are workshops and classes you'll be able to take to get better at different aspects of it, from software to accounting. See what your employer offers in terms of professional development and sign up for that with as much enthusiasm as you can muster. Also check to see what types of courses they'll help you pay for or what kinds of educational opportunities they'll reimburse you for. Put those on your to-do list. Everything you learn will add value to you as an employee—whether you stay with your current company, move on to another, or go out on your own.

You can also be strategic about where you put your time and money. Take a look at what skills the people above you on the pay scale have that you may lack. Take an even harder look at where your workplace has holes, either from someone leaving or from new technology or opportunities being added that no one is really on top of yet. Those should be top priority for you to learn.

Finally, think about what you already do well. How can you double down on it and get better? Or get certified? Or take a course that will set you up in a way that you'll be seen as an expert in that particular thing? Education is a powerful way to increase your perceived value, both where you currently are and to new employers or clients. Not everyone will care that you are, for instance, certified in Scrum (an agile project management system) or as a PMP (project management professional), but for the right employer, your certification might be the one thing that puts your application over the top.

Throughout this book, I talk a lot about different ways to make money, but I would say the cornerstone of any successful career is your own ability. Not just the ability to perform a particular job especially well, but also your ability to get in there and do any job with competence and integrity. In my own life, I have changed jobs multiple times and even changed careers more than once, but the skills I've brought with me have always seen me through each new situation. I care enough to learn what I don't know, I'm good with people (I'll talk more about that later), and I understand money and how to leverage it. I always do the best possible job, even if it means long hours, and I also know when to leave. I will work like the dickens, but I won't let others take advantage of me.

Integrity, commitment, a willingness to work hard, and a capacity to learn—these are invaluable no matter what you do. Using these skills to take advantage of the opportunities that come your way can set you up for professional and financial success.

Chapter Ten

Investment Choices

Investing is a whole new world for many people, but it's an important step to take. If you stuff your money in a mattress, you may know where it is all the time, but it's not going to be doing anything for you. In fact, it'll be slowly losing value as time goes on and prices go up.

Investing is making your money make money for you.

Investing in the Stock Market

We've already talked about how buying your own home can be a sound investment. Now, let's talk about stocks. There are several ways to invest in the stock market other than buying the stock yourself. If buying individual stocks makes you nervous, you can select the type of investment that offers you the best peace of mind with the greatest return. But you should at least consider getting in the game.

First, let me tell you what the stock market is NOT. It is not a get-rich-quick scheme. If you go in thinking you're going to make a million overnight, you are just waiting to be fleeced, either by some unscrupulous person waiting to sell you on a Ponzi scheme or by your own greed leading you to treat the stock market like a roulette wheel. Either way, you're going to lose your shirt—and possibly your home. I have known heirs to million-dollar fortunes who have blown through it in three years because they were sure they were smart enough, savvy enough, and lucky enough to double it overnight. Just because there is a risk in investing doesn't mean you're at the casino. It's not double-or-nothing.

Handling a Windfall

If you find yourself the beneficiary of an inheritance, a large insurance payout, or even a win from playing the ponies, don't blow it! I have known too many people who had sudden windfalls but had no structure for how to deal with their newfound money.

First of all, expect an endless stream of people to enter your life trying to take advantage of the situation. Don't fall for it. Money is a tool and, as such, it should be put to its best use and not abused.

Second, use this simple safety net: *Do nothing*. Don't spend it, don't invest it, just shove it in the bank or keep it in whatever form it's in (stocks, etc.) for a period of time while you figure things out. Here's what you'll want to do:

- Preserve the funds. Don't blow it all on risky investments. Save most of it and take out only a small amount to get started buying stocks or making other income-generating investments.

- If it's an inheritance, respect the benefactor's intentions.

- Don't go into unfamiliar areas. Now is not the time to be talked into buying a sheep farm in New Zealand or investing in modern art. Start with something you already know a little bit about and learn as you go.

- Evolve slowly. Think about what would genuinely change your life for the better, and for the long-term.

Slow, steady, and a long investment horizon—those are the keys to real wealth. And as that is the very attitude you need to make money in stocks, let's take a look at what the stock market is all about.

What Is the Dow Jones 30 Industrial Average?

The Dow Jones Industrial Average is a number you see bandied around a lot. It is the average stock price of thirty industrial stocks. In my opinion, there is excessive news about the rise and fall of the stock market looking at only this average. The reliance on the Dow Jones as a barometer for the economy is, I believe, overstated. In the last twenty years, almost half of the companies that once comprised the Dow are no longer listed as 2020 favorite stocks for one reason or another and have been taken out of the average. This means that the number shifts not necessarily because the foundations of our economy are going up and down, but because we can't decide for very long on what the foundations of our economy really are. To me, the Dow Jones 30 industrial stocks seem to be little more than cherry-picking.

That said, if you have to pick some stocks without necessarily understanding how their businesses work, you could do worse than to pick the ones followed by the Dow. Over a long period of time, the Dow has consistently gone up.

The key words here: *over a long period of time.*

In the short-term, just like individual stocks, the stocks making up the Dow will go up and then down and then back up. It's thirty different stocks, so that's more diversified than if you had all your money in just one or two stocks, but that doesn't mean it isn't subject to volatility. If you need the money soon, the stock market is not the safest place for it because Dow Jones stock may be in a recession. But if you have a long horizon for investing, you should certainly look into a diversified portfolio.

Standard and Poor's 500

Back when we were talking about your retirement, this is the type of index I meant when I referred to index funds. These are mutual funds that mirror an index such as the S&P 500, aligning your investment with the index. What that means is the holdings in the mutual fund are the same companies as those in the index. This means you can't beat the market, but you can't lose to it, either. Some days it'll go up, some days it'll go down, but over the long haul, you'll make almost a 10 percent return on investment—currently nearly five times what you can make with a certificate of deposit. There is risk, especially if you're looking at it as a short-term investment. But if you plan to let the money grow for the next couple of decades, an index fund might be worth looking into. You can buy shares directly from the mutual fund company or through your broker.

What's Going on Behind the Scenes?

It used to be that the approach to stock evaluation was based on a bull or bear market, meaning that the trend was going up or the trend was going down. So when you decided whether to buy or sell, it was largely based on the general flow of the market. Before television, before computers, you wouldn't necessarily see same-day results, much less minute-by-minute ups and downs unless you read financial newspapers. So decisions were made based on more general trends and information.

Some of the fundamentals that could cause a market change were things like the price-to-earnings ratio (P/E), which is the company's share price relative to its per-share earnings. In other words, how much it costs you to buy a share in the company compared to how much you can earn per share. It's not a one-to-one; sometimes the P/E on a company is very high because people believe the company will earn more in the future, so they're willing to pay more now. Valuations on P/E can be useful to help you compare companies that do very different things, because you're isolating just one piece of the puzzle.

It's worth reading some books on how to evaluate stocks, listening to experts talk about the market, and even learning the fundamentals of how the stock market works if you plan to invest in a serious way. This book is just an overview and not meant to tell you how to pick a stock. Also, as an aside, I had a brief, glorious, and ultimately disastrous experience as a day trader in my youth. From experience, I do not recommend this!

Let's go back to how things have historically worked in the stock market. In addition to P/E, movement in the market was governed by the Federal Reserve rates, unemployment rates, and political activity both in the country and around the world. These things are still true: You can see how the market reacts when reports or decisions are announced, or when there's a major world upheaval, such as when a new virus appears or a war breaks out. But in addition to that, we now have an instantaneous change of stock prices being processed through algorithms. Algorithmic trading is a method of executing orders using automated, preprogrammed trading instructions accounting for variables such as time, price, and volume to send small slices of the order out to the market over time.

Sound confusing? It is. And you don't need to know how it works. What you *do* need to know is what it leads to: Since so many stock consultants and other stock managers are establishing their trading by algorithms, there may be an exaggeration of the rise and fall of stocks. This is why over the course of a day, there are times when the market looks like a seesaw.

Here are the important things:

- Diversify. Don't put all your eggs in one basket, one company, or even one industry. Set yourself up to be able to make money in different ways.

- Do dollar cost averaging when possible. Invest a certain amount every month in something like an index fund or a series of stocks that you believe in. Spending a set amount on a regular basis means you buy more shares when the price is low (buy low!) and fewer shares when it goes up. It keeps you in the game.

- Have a long investment horizon. Over time, the stock market has reliably gone up, but on any given day or in any given year, it has been known to go down substantially. You can't time the market, so don't try. Don't put money in the stock market that you are going to absolutely need to spend in the next couple of years. When you're young, invest with a bias toward holding things for a decade or more. When you're nearing retirement or you think you'll need the money for something soon, start pulling it out of stocks and keeping it in safer investments, such as bonds or certificates of deposit.

- Get in the game. The stock market is a resource to grow your wealth. It's a way to make your money work for you. It's not the only way, but you shouldn't dismiss it out of hand just because it's complicated. At least learn enough to make an educated decision about whether or not investing in stocks, bonds, and mutual funds is a smart move for you.

Stocks

When you invest in stocks, you become an owner of the company you're investing in. You are held accountable as a stockholder for the good or bad things that can result from being a stockholder. You have a vote at stockholder meetings, and many activist investors have a voice. The more stock you own in a company, the more clout you have. Most people never own enough stock in a single company to shift how the company does business, but most people also don't want to become that involved. They don't have the time or expertise, and they often buy stock in the first place because they believe the board of directors is already doing a good job running things.

Stocks can make money for you in two ways. The first is *appreciation*. The advantage of owning shares in a company is that, as the company improves, grows larger, and becomes more valuable, the value of each share can go up. Let's say you bought one hundred shares when the price per share was $20. Your initial investment was $2,000. If you chose a good company whose value has increased, then after ten years, each share of stock is now selling for more money—let's say $30. Now, your investment is worth 100 x $30, or $3,000. That's a 50 percent increase in ten years. You picked a great company!

Of course, you might pick a company that's on the verge of collapse. If that happens, your one hundred shares may become worthless and you will have lost that initial $2,000 investment. This can happen! The stock market is not without risk. I've made money and I've lost money; you will, too. But there are ways to mitigate your risk.

The most important thing to do—and advice you've probably heard before picking up this book—is to diversify your portfolio. In simple terms, this means you want to own stocks not only in more than one company, but in more than one industry. Let's say you own stock in a company that makes widgets. You love widgets! You think the future of the world lies in widgets, and so you buy stock in two different companies that both make different but related widgets. That's terrific, but these should not be your only stocks. What happens if suddenly there's a shift in technology and the market for widgets dries up entirely?

If you also have stock in other industries, outside of widget manufacturing—say, healthcare, solar power, food, and entertainment—then a temporary or even permanent dip in one industry won't wipe out your life savings. Although I don't like to think of the stock market as a gambling den, in this case, one analogy is appropriate: Hedge your bets.

This is also where the idea of buying low and selling high comes in. Timing is your key to investment success. Markets go up (a bull market) and they also go down (a bear market)—but after they go down, they go back up. If your strategy is to hold stocks for the long-term, you should be fine. Eventually. But you'll be fine sooner if you bought when the market was low rather than at its recent height.

How can you do this?

That is a million-dollar question. People are paid vast sums of money to predict the movement of the market, whether it's on television or in newspapers or to their clients. But the truth is that, in the short run, no one knows where the market is going. You shouldn't try. What you should do, no matter where the market is today, is start looking for companies that you believe will continue to increase in value and make money in the long run. Those are the companies whose stock you want to buy, because no matter where they are now, you believe they will go up. That said, if you are lucky enough to be able to get into the market in the midst of a recession or after a catastrophic drop, such as the one prompted by the global pandemic we're going through as I write this, definitely get in the game. A friend of mine just called me to ask if now was the time for her to get into the stock market, and I said, oh yes! The market may still go down as I write this, but it will inevitably go back up.

This is what I mean by a long-term investment horizon. If you needed that money to live on today, it shouldn't have been in the stock market. You should have pulled it out three years ago. The money that you keep in the market is money you can afford to keep invested through good times and bad. The single worst mistake you can make is to sell when the market goes down. Maybe you can't buy, but you should at the very least hold.

The profitable investor picks long-term quality over hot issues or fads. Don't fall prey to the over-enthusiasm in a new product or hot company, which can drive up the share prices in the short-term but will eventually correct itself. The same is true for the entire market. There are times when the market seems to just keep going up and up, and investors keep buying, sometimes recklessly, because it seems like it will never go down. But it will. Try to invest in relatively low points in the market—and you can do this by setting aside the funds now. If you need to sell something in order to buy something, your goose is cooked because selling when the market seems to be going up every day is even harder than buying when everything is tumbling down. So set aside funds from your day job or side hustle on a regular basis so that you can invest whenever the moment is right.

Once again, be patient and hold out through the hard times. I really can't say this enough: The biggest mistake people make is panic-selling when the market starts to go down. Because it will go back up. This is why you shouldn't have money in the stock market that you're going to need in the short-term. If you are going to need those funds within the next few years, you should move your investments out of stocks and into safer investments, such as bonds or even certificates of deposit (CDs), which are like restricted savings accounts: In exchange for a better interest rate than your personal savings account will give you, you deposit a chunk of money in the bank that you are unable to touch for an agreed-upon amount of time (anything from several months to several years). You can even simply sell your stock and put the cash in your checking account if you're going to need it for, say, retirement or other living expenses. You never want to be forced into selling stock when the market is down just because you are desperate for money.

Another way to give yourself a safety net is through dollar cost averaging, which I talked about in terms of your retirement savings. Again, investing a set amount of money in stocks or mutual funds monthly smooths out the stock market bumps because you will buy more shares when the price is low and fewer when the price is high, but you will always be building your portfolio. It's an autopilot way to keep yourself in the game.

I mentioned that there are two ways a stock can provide money, and that second way is *dividends*. A dividend is a payment per share that the company can (but won't always) make. You can usually choose to take the dividend either in cash or use it to buy more shares of the stock (that's the "reinvest dividends" option).

It used to be that the primary way a company rewarded investors was through dividends, or regular payouts of money to its investors. If the share prices went up, that was of course a good thing, but most investors expected to see the return on their investment from dividends rather than by selling an appreciated stock. That's changed over time, although interestingly, stocks that pay dividends still tend to outperform stocks that don't, so looking for companies that directly share their profits with their investors may still be a good idea. (As always, the information I give is general and not meant to tell you what or how to buy. Please consult a professional if necessary, and always consult your own good sense.)

Depending upon the success of the company and how they wish to declare dividends (anything from monthly to annually), you will receive income from your stocks on a regular basis. One thing you should consider is the "reinvest dividends" option I mentioned earlier. What this means is that you use your dividends to buy more shares of that particular stock. Since dividends are paid per share owned, that means the next time they pay out, you'll get a little more money because you'll own a few more shares. Obviously, it's not an exact science: Dividend payments can vary wildly even within a company, depending on how the economy is doing, but if you don't need the cash now, it's a painless way to keep investing in your future and worth considering.

Choosing a Broker

Before we talk about picking stocks, I want to talk about picking a stock broker. When you're deciding who to work with as your broker, it's like you're picking a friend and potential business partner. You want to make sure you have a good rapport, that you really understand one another. Your relationship, the click between you, is very important. But you also want to do a little checking around. You want someone who knows what they're doing because you're going to be relying on them for expert guidance and advice, and possibly with your life savings.

You want to make sure the broker graduated college, and that they majored in finance. You don't want someone who is just a salesperson, someone who was selling cars last week and this week is selling you on stocks and bonds. You want someone who knows the market and understands the many variables that go into putting a portfolio together. While you want someone you get along with, they are, at heart, a consultant, not a friend. And as a consultant, they will be in a position to steer you, for better or for worse. So check your gut, but also check with the Better Business Bureau.

Do you like the broker? You also want to feel that you can hold your own in a conversation. Yes, you want their guidance and advice, but you don't want to get pushed around.

You should also look at the brokerage house itself. It should be more than just a cubbyhole in a building, because you're not just choosing the broker—you're also partnering with the company that has the broker's license on the exchange. Are they in trouble? Have they been sued?

There are unscrupulous people out there. I don't mean for you to stuff your money in your mattress, but you have to be mentally prepared for the possibility that you can be swindled. No one, not even me, is smart enough to spot a crooked broker from fifty feet away. I've been taken in by friends of friends, by neighbors, by the guy with the ready smile and frank gaze at the club who proceeds to steer me toward investments that make money for him. It happened less and less over the years as I got wiser and learned from my mistakes, but don't think it can't happen to you. And don't be afraid to do something about it.

I've had people come to me with the worst stories. I knew an older woman who came to me in a panic. "Robert," she said, "I put all my savings with my broker, and he said the best thing for me is bonds." I told her yes, absolutely, at her age, bonds were the safest choice. "But," she said, "it's all gone! All my money is gone." So I looked over the bonds he had sold her.

But first, a quick lesson: What is a bond?

Bonds

You actually already know what bonds are because you've probably voted on government bond issues in your neighborhood to fund various projects. You may even have bought bonds already. U.S. government bonds called Series I and Series EE are attractive ways for parents and grandparents to set aside some funds for college for their children or grandchildren because the interest on the bonds is tax-free when used to pay college tuition. (Note: As always, talk to your own tax professional about your exact situation. This isn't professional tax advice tailored to you.) In general, bonds are a very secure investment.

At heart, a bond is an IOU. You give the government or utility company or corporation money that they promise to repay with interest. Many types of bonds are backed by different government entities, including federal, state, and municipal, along with quasi-government entities such as utility companies. A large number of bonds are sold by corporations.

The bonds have a face value, due date, and interest rate. The purchase price can vary depending on the interest rate offered and how far off the due date is. Bonds can be sold at face value, at a discount, or at premium value (more than the face value of the bond). All of this depends on the security backing of the bond and the market conditions. If the stated interest rate on the bond is a better return than the market rate, the bond will be sold at a premium with the expectation that you can make more money on it over time than you would elsewhere. If the stated interest rate is lower than market rate, the bond will be discounted. What must be considered is the face value for which the bond will be paid off. The amount paid on the due date will more than likely not have the dollar value when purchased.

This is a little tricky to understand, but the idea is that the dollar you invest in buying the bond is worth less by the time the bond is paid back to you. We all know a dollar doesn't buy what it used to; this is the exact same idea. For an investment to be worth making, it has to keep the value of the money you paid for it, not just return the literal number of dollars you put in. So the interest rate needs to be better than inflation, at a bare minimum.

Back to my friend, whose broker had convinced her to put all her money in bonds. While that was a safe investment—and if she'd looked it up or asked a friend like me, everyone would have agreed that at her age, bonds were much safer than the stock market—the problem was that the only bonds he'd given her had been ones available at a tremendous discount, up to 50 percent off. He probably sold her on what a deal she'd be getting—look at how her money could double! But I'll tell you why these bonds were so cheap: They were junk bonds.

A junk bond is a very risky investment because there's a good chance that the entity issuing the bond is going to default on the loan. These are companies that are already in financial trouble and there's a very good chance they won't be able to turn it around, even with the money raised by issuing bonds. This means not only will they not pay the promised interest rate on the bond, but they won't pay back the principal, either. My friend's broker had off-loaded abandoned mines, struggling utilities companies, and similar bad debts on her.

Now, I could have fixed this for her. I offered to. I told her I could get her money back by writing the brokerage firm a letter outlining the situation. She had no experience in investing and the broker had clearly taken advantage of her in a way that was completely unethical. But—and here's the real tragedy—she wouldn't let me do it. She was afraid her daughter-in-law would find out and think she was incompetent. She would rather actually lose all her money than be thought incompetent of taking care of her own finances.

And it's not just her—everyone, to some extent, will cover up a bad decision rather than being thought stupid or incompetent or naïve. As human beings, it stabs right in the heart of our own self-image, our self-esteem. But I'm going to tell you right now that you have to be willing to admit to making a mistake. Because if you aren't, all that does is protect the crooks and hurt you. Being unwilling to face a situation because you're afraid of looking bad means you'll never learn from it. It can also make you even more willing to take crazy risks to try to "make up" the money you lost the first time. It can make you even easier to swindle again. And it's not good for you, money aside. Financial stability is about freedom; why be the type of person who trades their freedom for a façade of looking good to others? Admit the mistake, fix what you can, learn from it, and move on.

And always remember, if it looks too good to be true, it is.

Discount Brokers

"But Robert," I can hear some of you say, "I don't have $100,000 to invest with a broker. How can I get in the stock market and get the help I need?" Luckily, there are several ways. For some mutual funds, and particularly for IRAs, you can set up an account directly with the company offering the mutual fund. For your 401(k), which you should definitely take full advantage of, you can set up an account through your employer.

Another way to get into the stock market with a small starting investment is to open an account with a discount broker. I personally have two accounts with discount brokers. They broke the mold when they came on the scene, offering an opportunity for small investors to get into the stock market and creating a low-fee model.

Discount brokers will have all the charts and information I talked about earlier. My only real piece of advice on this is to go with someone local; you want to be able to walk into the office and talk to a real person. I know we're in a virtually connected world, but me, I like face-to-face contact. I read people and their personalities so much better when I'm with them, when I can see their faces. You want to be able to talk to a broker about a stock you're considering and get their opinion and the reports and paperwork on them that I discussed. You still have to like and trust the broker, so make a couple of appointments with different ones in your area. Meet them and learn.

And don't be shy about asking questions. Ask them the criteria for what you should be buying. Have them help you pick out some stocks. Be a nuisance and be willing to learn. The worst attitude is to go in like an expert. Don't try to look like you know it all. Those are the biggest fools—the ones who need to believe they have nothing left to learn.

Chapter Eleven

Picking Stocks

The single most important piece of advice you can take from me is to *manage your risk*. Have a long-term investment horizon and reasonable expectations. You are not going to make money overnight, and you shouldn't need to.

I always supported my family off of my salary. My side business earned money that went into investing. At my late wife, Bernice's, urging, I quit working for someone else entirely. I took my own advice to invest my time and energies in the family business. The money we put into the stock market was always seen as icing on the cake. It's not the cake itself. This is not money you should need to live day to day. This is your investment in the future, your safety net in retirement, your freedom to change jobs or take a risk that your 9-to-5 doesn't provide. Don't put yourself in a situation where you're desperate for the returns you may or may not see for years down the line. It will make you reckless, and that will make you broke.

On that note, I want to talk a little about the IPO, or initial public offering. Many big houses underwrite the initial investment in a firm, which means the IPO of a company may look solid, it may even look amazing, but it may not have any stability. You don't know if it does or not, because it's brand-new. Of course the IPOs you hear about are the ones that were amazing, but that doesn't mean they all become Apple or Starbucks or Tesla. A lot of them don't, and you don't really hear much about those investors losing their money, do you? If you have the idea that an IPO will make you rich overnight, forget it. That is the exact wrong headspace for investing in the stock market. You don't want an IPO. You want security. You don't want to be a speculator; you want to be an investor.

Invest in the stock market with a plan for five years or more. Don't invest more than you can afford to lose so that if something happens to that investment, your whole life is not ruined. Remember, stock is the icing on the cake. The cake is your employment, it's your career, it's money from investments you can count on. Stocks can be your safety net.

Evaluating Stocks

In order to wisely pick a stock, you'll need to do some homework. Where do you find the information to evaluate a stock? Every company is required to offer information on their stock to you, by law. Read it. This standardized information, the Price/Earnings statement, and the balance sheet, in particular, allow you to compare companies, apples to apples. It doesn't matter if they make shoes or computer chips or movies; looking at this information will give you a basis to compare different companies.

Reading these reports may seem like a lot of work, and it is. You're new at it. You don't know what you're looking at yet, but this is how you learn. This is something your broker can help you understand. Never skip this step. If you get a hot lead, if a stock is recommended, if the media or your friends or someone at the office is enthusiastic about it—that kind of gossip is baloney. Do the research. Because no matter how attractive a stock looks today, no matter how much buzz it's getting in the press, other factors are at play.

Things to Avoid in a Stock

Here are some factors to think about when picking stocks. The first list I'm going to give you, below, describes the things you should *watch out for*. They are bad for the company, for the stock value, and for your investment in the long run. The second list, in the next section, points out things you *want* in a stock.

Here's what will sink a stock in the long run:

- **Volatility.** If the stock is exhibiting volatility, then buying it means taking a risk. There are so many companies out there that are volatile by their nature. They go up and down at the slightest change. Let other people invest in those. You're looking for stability. Look at the chart of what the stock has been doing over time—and that time should be at least the last five years. You really don't want anything newer than that because there's no history for you to evaluate. It's all promises and castles in the air. So look at the chart of what the stock has done over the last several years. Does it look like a seesaw? Don't ever think you'll be so smart as to pick it at the bottom.

   Obviously, if the market itself has taken a major hit during that time—the 2008 recession, the current pandemic—you will see that reflected. What you're looking for is a down-and-up pattern that you don't see everywhere else. One that doesn't have "global pandemic" as the reason. If you see that seesaw pattern, it means the stock is volatile, and the reason it's volatile is that something is happening inside the company itself. It's something that they're doing. You want to see a straight line going up year after year. An upward trend.

   Now, sometimes you'll see a stock that was mostly upward, but there was an unexplained downturn here or there. Ask why. Do some research. Did the market for their product change? No one is driving stagecoaches anymore; the companies that made them had to pivot or go out of business. Is that the problem? Is there new management? Don't think that just because a company was once a safe bet that it will continue to be so forever. If it's up and down now, don't buy the stock no matter what it used to look like.

- **Bad press.** Look, any kind of news about a company can create swings in the value of their stock, both gains and losses. "The market overreacted" is one set of news, and yes, that does happen, but let's take a good look at why the market reacted in the first place. If the company was massively profitable, but then stories came out about them lying about their products—don't touch it. It's not a great company; it's a company that's great at fooling people. What about things that are impacted by change in our understanding or in people's values? With climate change talked about daily, why would you invest in coal? Mad cow disease made beef a very poor investment. Fur is another thing; whatever your personal feeling about it, there has been a tipping point about the advisability of showing up draped in fur. Plus, there's been a shift in our culture: Middle-class men no longer gift their wives with fur coats. It's not a thing anymore the way it was fifty or sixty years ago.

Also, you have to be very wary of thinking something like, "Well, sure, they took a loss because of this set of circumstances, but that's okay, they could come back from that. Look how much money they made last year!" Good luck with that! Sure, they may come back, but it's going to be an uphill battle and why should you take the risk? There are a lot of stable, reliable companies where you have a better chance of making steady money over the long haul. Don't give into the rush of trying to make money hand over fist. There is no point, especially for a young, beginning investor, in taking a chance on something that's being talked about. News can give you one hell of a loss.

- **Issues with high debt structure to capital.** What does this mean, exactly? There are many companies that thrive by taking huge loans to fund their growth and then paying interest on those loans. What this means is if they have a good year, that profit is to some extent an illusion because a good portion of it has to go to paying the interest on their debt, or even paying down some of the principal. But when they have a bad year, they will still have to pay both the debt and the interest on that debt. It can be crippling. And if their answer is to borrow more, to go more deeply in debt, they are in real trouble for the long haul—which, remember, is all you care about. This is where having a broker you can trust to talk it over with can be invaluable. In general, remember that a heavy debt structure means that if something goes wrong, it will go *very* wrong.

- **Issues with low return on capital.** Here, you're looking at how much the company invested in their infrastructure, in being able to produce or create whatever the company has promised to create. And then you're seeing what value they've actually been able to create with all of that investment.

For instance, let's go back to widgets. Let's say there's a widget company that for years bought a lot of machinery and built a plant, all with the idea that they would make a lot of widgets. After all that investment, what are you getting for it? How many widgets can they create and what's the real market for them? How much are they worth? When will this enormous investment, all the money they poured into it to ramp up, pay off? The answer is never, if they are undercapitalized.

They may have borrowed so much money that they can look like they're doing well because they have a large cash balance, but they don't make a profit on that debt. They are actually just coasting on borrowed money—which will eventually have to be paid back. Also be wary of companies that are heavy on inventory, things they're just holding onto. It doesn't matter how much profit they stand to make; inventory isn't worth anything if they can't sell it. You want to avoid a company that has a lot of debt and not enough cash coming in, because what you really don't want is for them to have to borrow more in order to grow. You want them to be bringing in enough cash and making enough profit that they can grow their business themselves.

Here's one way to look at it: Let's say you have an old clunker of a car. Your neighbor also has a clunker, but he decides to go out and buy a brand-new car. People who are judging you just by the cars parked in your driveways might say, "Wow, your neighbor is rich!" But here's the thing: He bought that new car on credit. Meanwhile, you don't have a new car, you don't look rich from the outside, but you also don't have the debt your neighbor now carries. That new car is an illusion of wealth, not the real thing.

The same is true with companies. A company may build a new plant or rent swanky offices or carry a lot of inventory. They give the appearance of being prosperous, but they have an awful lot of debt. So when you're evaluating a company, you have to see if they really are growing like mad or have created the illusion of growth by overborrowing. They may be shiny and new, and even have cash coming in, but if they have a large debt underpinning it, it's not real. They may make a lot of stuff, they may have all this inventory, but if it doesn't sell, they're not really prosperous.

Back in the day, I knew a guy with a business of selling encyclopedias door to door. The problem was he sold them on credit, which meant people promised to pay eventually, but there was no real cash flow. He had the appearance of prosperity, but it was all a puff of smoke. His company went broke the way a lot of companies go broke—they were doing stupid things to try to look good, to lure people into buying stock. But that kind of scheme eventually falls apart. You don't want to be caught in the rubble when it collapses.

- **Issues with low cash to capital.** Let's look at a retailer. As I write this, many old, trusted names in retailing have gone into bankruptcy over the last few years. How is that possible? I'll tell you how. They started a credit system. As soon as I hear of a retailer offering their own line of credit, I know there will be problems down the road because they'll no longer see their profits in selling the goods, but in the interest on the credit fees they charged. Once they start issuing their own credit, they quickly discover that they make more profit on financing purchases than they do from the item itself. It can swell their profits—on paper. But the problem with selling credit is that the company doesn't really have that money until the customer pays them. In other words, you go home with a washing machine, but they don't actually get the money to cover the costs of that washing machine, much less make a profit on it, until you pay them back. And just like with junk bonds, not everyone pays the interest or principal that they owe.

The retailers who have gone into bankruptcy didn't really have cash coming in. They had competition for credit and a lack of cash flow, which brought them down. They were relying on the customers to pay them someday. Be wary: Any company that's built on credit is a risk. A recession means that suddenly a lot of people are without jobs and unable or unwilling to pay their credit card debt. Whether you're selling a toaster or a car, if you're providing the credit directly to your customers, you're at risk. Our country is big on credit, but when people can't pay and you're out the inventory you sold them, things can go downhill fast.

- **Issues with minimal dividends giving poor returns.** I like dividends. I like companies that share profits with investors as soon as they can. If they don't give you anything over the years, why are you there? You want to invest in a company that gives a 4 percent, 5 percent, even 8 percent dividend over the years. You want to at least do better than inflation, and you definitely don't want your only reward for investing to be the price per share going up—because sometimes it will go down. You will pay taxes on dividends, of course (and you should talk to your tax advisor about that), but regular dividends are your insurance that the company you invested in is doing well. You don't want a company that harbors all their profit and never gives you anything but some promise of future profits. There always has to be a balance: Some profit gets reinvested in the company, and some gets distributed to those who bought the shares that fueled the growth.

Things You Want in a Stock

Now you know the things that should make you think twice about investing in a particular company by buying their stock. Here, on the other hand, is the list of good things to look for in a stock, things that will be beneficial for the company and for you in the long run:

- **Issues with five or more years of increasing dividends.** Again, you don't want a new company, something only a year or two old. That's really not enough time to know how they're doing; you want to see how their management navigates the bad times as well as the good. But if they've been around a while and you can see that they continue to pay dividends on a regular basis, and those dividends have increased over time, that's a good indication that this is a stock that will be able to make you money.

- **Issues with better than average price-to-earnings ratio.** The

P/E is simply the price that you pay per share of stock over the per-share earnings of the company. It's the cost of the stock over the value that share represents. This is where it's important to see what the P/E of other companies might be. Both the S&P 500 and Dow Jones have a P/E ratio, and you can see charts of their P/E over the years so you can compare your stock to the market as a whole. Again, I think the Dow Jones cherry-picks—not that they're not good stocks, they often are, but they change over time. Still, it can give you some context for a company's P/E numbers. A high P/E ratio can mean that investors expect the company to earn more in the future, but it can also mean that the company is overvalued.

Get advice from your broker and also use your own judgment about whether or not a company is sound. I have a friend who only ever buys stock in products he personally likes and uses. It's an approach that's made him a lot of money. I don't think that's the only thing you should look at, but I do think you should factor it in.

- **Good branding/name recommendation.** Let's face it, you don't just buy a product—you buy the brand. You buy the promise that they make and the way they make you feel. For instance, I only buy a Gillette razor. I like the blade. I saw stores with shelves of Gillette products, and I figured other men also recognized and trusted the Gillette name. So I bought Gillette stock. A company's brand creates a bond with customers. It creates good will. If they deliver on one product you've tried, you're more likely to buy another one of their products—and if you will, so will others. Then, of course, once you buy their stock, you'll buy even more of their product, or buy it exclusively, because you want to support the company you've invested in.

This is a very good way to pick your first stock. There are thousands of stocks out there, and it can be overwhelming. You might even think, "How do I have the gall to think I can pick a good stock?" Start with what you like and trust.

- **Issues with a strong cash income to debt structure.** This one really takes digging into. It may be that the company doesn't show a lot of profit. The income may be really squeezed year to year because, let's say, they keep expanding, but it can still be good in the long run as long as the cash keeps coming in. If they have a good flow of cash coming in, even when they're not seeing a profit, that's still better than having a false profit because they keep taking out loans. They can have debt so long as the debt isn't so powerful that it sucks up all the cash.

Minimizing Risk

These factors that affect stocks are the kinds of things you'll have to talk over with your broker, which is why you need someone who knows what they're talking about. Company-issued reports are a start, but remember that reports are only as good as the integrity of the person writing them. Not that I'm saying they're liars, just that everyone wants to put their best foot forward. Assume all projections are optimistic. Don't get caught up in the enthusiasm of a sales pitch.

Look at three things:

- The cash flow

- The profit/loss statement

- The balance sheet

Talk to your broker and learn to read between the lines. Never be afraid to ask questions—lots of them. Listen to the answers, get better at evaluating reports, and try to limit your mistakes by not putting all your eggs into one basket (or junk bonds).

Investing is always a risk. You can minimize your risk by researching, by diversifying, by putting a little in on a steady basis. Risk can be good, if you know how to manage it. You never throw everything you have at a stock or a piece of real estate or a new business. You take things one step at a time and you have a backup plan. It's not a risk in and of itself to invest in anything, whether it's the stock market or buying a restaurant. It's good money management to take the opportunities that are available to you, and it's a waste not to use your money to make money. Just don't put yourself in a situation where you can't afford to lose your stake.

Don't Quit at the Bottom

Dollar cost averaging is one of the best things that most people can do. It's a systematic investment. You get to take advantage of opportunities and downswings without even thinking about it. But timing is also important. You can't let fear keep you from investing when the market is down. It's an opportunity to invest, not a sign to pull out. I really can't say this enough: DON'T QUIT AT THE BOTTOM! That is a breakdown in thinking—it's being driven by your fear that you have to get what you can when there's still a few pennies to get. NO! It's the opposite.

Growing up, I knew a man who bought everything he could during the Great Depression. He bought and held stocks that resurged and made him wealthy, and he's not alone. The people who didn't sell during those years, even if they didn't buy, still saw their wealth return. Psychologically, it can be tough, but it's much easier when you don't need the money you invested for at least two years out. Having a long investment horizon, which you can do when you count on your own abilities and your career to meet your day-to-day needs, can prevent you from panicking when the market goes down.

Do everything cautiously, step by step. Pick your stocks. Buy a little every month. Bide your time. If something unexpected happens and there's a shock to the economy—like, for instance, a global pandemic—and the market falls, be ready to move in. Because pandemics will end and the market will resurge.

Never put your full faith—or all your cash—in anything, much less the stock market. Don't get sucked into "I'm going to get rich." Think instead, "I'm growing with the system." I feel really good in my heart that despite the current upheaval, the country is doing well. People are resilient. When we go through a bad time, we don't quit; we stay with it. So don't pull out when the market is down.

Last year I made over 30 percent on my investments—and I had fun doing it! Right now, I'm staying exactly where I am. The market is being held by government intervention, which will lead to recession and inflation. Stay nimble. The market is down by a third as I write this, but I'm not selling, because I believe the pandemic will end and everything will come back. I'm in my eighties, and I still have a long investment horizon! Panic is a poor advisor. Don't ever do anything drastic.

As for getting into the market in the first place, I know it can be daunting. It can take a long time to feel comfortable picking stocks. Don't rush things. Study the stock market, read analyses, look for companies whose products you use and love and dip your toe in the water. The internet has made it possible for you to learn a lot and to follow a stock from your own home, your own phone! You have many more tools available than I did, when I would get up at dawn to be at my broker's at 6:00 a.m.; I'd watch the board there, where they posted the latest information, for an hour before going into work. If I can do that to learn the ropes, then checking your phone is well within your wheelhouse!

Or you may decide you don't want to pick stocks yourself. That's fine, too. You have options.

Having Someone Else Manage Your Money

Not everyone is interested in learning how to buy and sell stocks. If you want someone else to take charge of your money, you can hire a financial service. But you can also invest directly in either a mutual fund or an exchange traded fund through an online, discount broker. First, let's look at hiring someone to do your investing for you.

A financial service will often take care of a number of financial issues, from investments to estate planning to taxes. They also generally come with a required initial asset management threshold of several hundred thousand dollars. If you're young and just starting out, you may not meet their baseline investment limit, but you also may not need it. A financial service could, however, be the right way to help your parents figure out how to manage their assets.

Of course you will check up on any financial service first. You want to make sure it's not some fly-by-night company, or someone unscrupulous. You should also make sure they know what they're doing. Meet them in person, ask a lot of questions, and take the time to learn their results:

- Have they had the right formal education?

- Are their goals aligned with your goals?

- Are you regularly consulted?

- How long has the company been in business?

- Do you understand their reports?

Due diligence can keep you from trusting the wrong people and losing your shirt. Remember that Bernie Madoff's name is now synonymous with being swindled. I'm not telling you this to scare you away from hiring a financial manager. I just want you to keep in mind that the hallmark of a con is that it sounds too good to be true. Think of my friend and her 50-percent-off "investment" in junk bonds. My own motto is "Trust, but verify." Do your homework, talk to people, check with the Better Business Bureau, and run the other way if something sounds like manna from heaven. No one should ever sell you on the idea that they can make you rich quickly.

The easiest way to invest in the stock market (with trained professionals) is to invest in mutual funds or exchanged traded funds.

Mutual Funds

Like with a stock, you want to invest in a fund that's been around a while. New mutual funds are too tricky to evaluate. There are funds whose results can be deceptive; they may do extremely well for a short period of time due to a particular strategy, and some are highly marketed. This is one of those times when you don't want to listen to the buzz. With funds, you can compare apples to apples by evaluating the net results of a fund over a ten-year history. Anything less can be misleading. There's an old adage "Figures don't lie, but liars figure." Not that I'm suggesting they're lying on purpose, but merely that they will, of course, want to show off to their best advantage. A fund without a history has no real foundation for you to make a good decision. Once again, a long investment horizon is your friend because it allows you to withstand a down market. Historically, the market has always gone up eventually.

For a mutual fund, you will have the option of choosing an actively traded fund or a passive fund, which seeks only to mimic the stock market. Evaluate your options, but keep this in mind: Actively traded funds have more fees, so make sure you factor that in when you look at the returns each one offers. Past returns are useful information, but no guarantee of future returns. There is also a kind of fund I mentioned earlier, known as a "target date" fund, which moves you into more conservative investments the closer you get to retirement. Boy, talk about making things easy on a new investor! If you have no interest at all in keeping tabs on your investments, you might consider something like this that does everything for you automatically. As always, arranging for automatic monthly payments into the fund sets you up to put dollar cost averaging to work for you.

Can it really be that easy? Yes, it can. But you have to make the decision, set it up, take the plunge. Ten years from now, you don't want to regret not having started today.

Exchange Traded Funds

The other type of investment under management that I mentioned is an exchange traded fund (ETF). It used to be that I invariably suggested people should buy mutual funds, particularly if they are new to the stock market or not too interested in picking stocks. There are ongoing fees involved, but since the fund managers are doing all the thinking for you, it's a pretty good deal. And dollar cost averaging with a fund is easy; you can automatically put in a limited sum every month. But more recently, another system has developed: ETFs. With an ETF, you pay the fee one time to buy shares, just as you would to trade a stock, but you never have to pay a fee again.

An ETF tracks an index, a commodity, or a basket of assets like an index fund while it also trades like a stock on an exchange. So it's a little like a mutual fund, except that it's actually traded like a stock. Prices may fluctuate throughout the day. Owning ETFs gives you the diversification of an index fund as well as the ability to sell short, buy on margin, and purchase as little as one share. While some ETFs give you broad diversification, others are sector ETFs, which give you a narrow slice of the market by industry, such as medical technology or energy. Be careful, because that focus is riskier than a wide, diverse portfolio, but with the risk comes the greater potential for reward.

I might sound like a broken record, but a long investment horizon and careful, slow investment with dollar cost averaging can minimize the risk. As always, you need to look at what you're comfortable with and what you can afford to lose. If you think, "Ah, yes! This is how I'll get rich quick!"—stay out of the market! You'll make terrible decisions with that attitude.

The Benefits of Being Cautious

Every so often, someone I know asks me for advice. I always give the best advice I can, and then I let them take it or not. You're an adult and I let you go and make your own mistakes.

We are in a prosperous period when people may win the lottery or come into a substantial inheritance, insurance payout, settlement, etc. The recipient is not accustomed to dealing with sudden wealth. Too many times they find new friends, relatives, and investment advisors

STOCKS

REPRESENT SHAREHOLDER IN A COMPANY

ADVANTAGES
- LARGE POTENTIAL FOR GAINS
- EASY TO BUY AND SELL
- STAY AHEAD OF INFLATION
- NO TAXES ON GAINS UNTIL YOU SELL

DISADVANTAGES
- RISK OF EXTREME LOSS
- TRADING AND OTHER FEES
- NO GUARANTEED RETURN

BONDS

REPRESENT DEBT FOR A COMPANY

ADVANTAGES
- STEADY GUARANTEED RETURNS
- CLEAR CREDIT RATINGS
- PAID BEFORE SHAREHOLDERS IN A LIQUIDATION

DISADVANTAGES
- FLUCTUATE WITH INTEREST RATES
- MAY SELL AT DISCOUNT BEFORE MATURITY
- USUALLY LOWER RETURNS THAN EQUITY HOLDERS

BUILDING WEALTH 101

ADVANTAGES
DIVIDENDS REINVESTED
FUND MANAGERS CREATE PORTFOLIOS
DIVERSIFICATION MINIMIZES RISK

MUTUAL FUNDS

DISADVANTAGES
MANAGEMENT FEES
NO CONTROL OVER PORTFOLIO

A VARIETY OF STOCK, BONDS, AND OTHER INVESTMENTS IN ONE MUTUAL

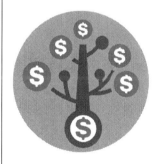

ADVANTAGES
DIVIDENDS REINVESTED
EASY TO TRADE
LIMITED CAPITAL GAINS TAXES
DIVERSIFICATION MINIMIZES RISK

ETFs
(EXCHANGE TRADED FUNDS)

DISADVANTAGES
FEES
BROKER COMMISSIONS
LOWER RETURNS THAN OTHERS

A VARIETY OF STOCK, BONDS, AND OTHER INVESTMENTS IN ONE FUND

to influence how they manage their new wealth and too many times it is selfish advice. The sudden wealth disappears within several years. Prudence is overcome with false illusions. It is said, "It's harder to keep it than make it."

The first step is having your newly acquired wealth (your nest egg) placed into a savings account. Settle down for several months and consider allocating your options. That's right. It's budget time again. Develop a long-term frame of mind to make the most of your nest egg. What will the new you do regarding your lifestyle, investing, and contributing to heirs and charitable causes?

It is nauseating to see a fool and his money. Extravagance is short-lived and so wasteful—especially when you can add benefit rather than deplete it. From wherever the nest egg came, it would be ungrateful not to use it wisely.

This book is about building wealth. With caution, you can build even more wealth. It takes special consideration to fulfill all sensible options. My suggestion is to take small steps and experience the outcome.

Once you determine your investment allocation—either in stock, real estate, or business—only invest a minimum amount and assay the outcome. As you progress, add another portion and see what is happening. Sudden growth or setbacks are common. At first you can never be too cautious. It takes experience to make the right choices. You are in for the longterm, so it takes time and patience.

It is not greedy or hoarding to preserve capital. When you have capital, you are building wealth and wealth begets wealth. Here is the best part: Now you can do the great things you always wanted. If you liked your job before, keep it. If you can be productive in another way, go for it. You have your capital to back you up and a new peace of mind.

Chapter Twelve

Death and Taxes

This may not be your favorite chapter, but it's definitely not one you should skip. Death and taxes are two things you can't skip in real life. The real danger from both of them is to not plan for them. A lifetime of work can be undone in an instant if something happens to you and you haven't taken steps to mitigate the impact on your family.

Don't be a selfish oaf. Handle things now, and then you can relax and not think about it again because you know your loved ones (and your business) will be taken care of.

Life Insurance

Life insurance is about protection. In the event of your death, it keeps your family or company from losing the economic value you provide. Nothing will ever replace your value to them as a loved one or partner or guiding light, but not having to worry about money in the event of your death is a final gift you can give them. Not to be macabre, but life insurance should really be called death insurance—but although that's more accurate, it would sell fewer policies!

Insurance companies make money by having as wide a span of

policyholders as possible. This spreads out the risk. You pay a monthly premium that is structured along the lines of statistical probabilities.

There are two kinds of life insurance: whole life and term. Both are basically what they sound like. Whole life insurance covers you for your whole life, while term is written to cover a period of years, anything from five to ten to twenty-five years.

The monthly premium for term insurance is cheaper than for whole life for a couple of reasons. First, it doesn't last forever. It will only pay out if you die within the term it covers. New parents will get term insurance to cover their child's youth through college because the loss of one parent during that time can be so devastating economically as well as emotionally. I'm not just talking about the breadwinner, either. First, most households today have two income-earners, and second, you just try to replace everything a stay-at-home parent does! Do you really want your family to have to go through financial as well as emotional stress if something happens to you? If you have children, don't stint on life insurance.

The second reason that term insurance is cheaper is that whole life builds in a cash value to your policy. Think of it as a forced savings plan. Every premium payment has a portion of money that goes into a savings account for you. At any point, you can borrow on your whole life policy or even cash it in if you no longer need it. Term insurance, on the other hand, is only written to pay out in the eventuality of your death. When the term ends, the policy collapses. It is strictly for emergencies, not a vehicle for savings.

One type of life insurance isn't better than the other. It's a matter of choice, what you can afford, and what makes the most sense for you. With the caveat that you need to look at your unique situation and make decisions that work for you, here are some guidelines.

First, the premium should be 1 percent of your net income. So if you bring home $5,000 a month, you can afford about $50 per month for the policy. The policy is based on both your profile (age/health/gender) and how much money it will pay in the event of your death; you can't control the first (except by doing smart things like not smoking!), but of course you can determine how much coverage you want to purchase.

That's my second suggestion: Look at what you want your family to be able to afford if something happens to you. Some people only have life insurance to cover their funeral costs, and while that's better than nothing, wouldn't you rather your family didn't lose their home? To me, that's the bare minimum coverage you need: How much debt are you carrying on your home? What would it take to pay off your mortgage? Cover that much, and both you and your family can rest easy. You may not be able to afford whole life; that's what term is there for. If proper protection is still more than 1 percent of your income, it may take cutting back a bit somewhere else, but it's 100 percent worth it.

Timing matters here, too. Get life insurance as early as possible so that the premium is lower. As you will never be as young as you are now, get it as soon as possible no matter how old you are. Of course, if it's whole life, you have to pay premiums for a longer period of time, but here's the thing: The premium remains the same; it's not tied to and adjusted for inflation. Which means ten years from now, you'll be paying the same amount, but you'll be paying it with cheaper dollars. What more do you want?

My intention here is not that you sacrifice for insurance, but I sure do intend to keep you from ignoring the contingency. Insurance is there so you can deal with it once and then forget it. Pay the premiums by auto-pay every month. Make sure the policy is somewhere your family can find it if something happens to you, and then forget it! Pat yourself on the back that you are a responsible adult and go live a great life. That's what insurance gives you—that peace of mind that lets you be your best self.

For any responsibilities you have, you must think of the nest egg of insurance to cover those responsibilities if you're not there. For many business owners, their assets are all tied up in their business; if they died without insurance, there would be no real money—which means the company might have to be collapsed in order to pay the estate taxes. Don't let that happen to your life's work. Having insurance is good budgeting and good management. I don't believe you should think of it as being excessive or extra, but instead think of it as a necessity. I recommend having insurance even before you start building a stock portfolio.

I've had friends say, "Robert, insurance is a waste of money! I can just put money aside for my family. I'll invest it instead—that's a much better use of the money." Yeah, sure, you could. But here's the truth: You won't! If you're not forced to set that money aside by paying premiums, you will splurge on a vacation or blow $50 a month on lattes (with coffee prices what they are, that's easy to do). And because you are selfish and don't want to face your own mortality and you kid yourself that you're smarter than everyone else, if something did happen to you, your family's security would be destroyed.

Buy the policy.

I have millions of dollars of insurance on my own life. I love it. It gives me so much peace of mind to know that my family, my businesses, and my legacy will keep on going strong after I'm gone. From the time I was first married, I always went into buying insurance with the idea that what I really wanted to protect was the house. I had a different policy for every mortgage I had in order to make sure my family didn't lose their home. When we started to buy properties to rent out, apartment complexes, I did the same thing. I always saw it as a business expense. It takes a lot of the insecurity and angst out of buying a property, because if something terrible happened, my family wouldn't have to scramble to sell. If you want to cover college expenses, here again, you might want to buy another policy, such as annuity to cash in for college tuition.

For my businesses, I have a key man policy, which is life insurance on a key person that the business depends upon. In cases like that, the company can buy the insurance, pay the premium, and be the beneficiary of the policy. This is a good moment to point out that you always have the option to decide who the beneficiary is going to be. The insurance is on your life, you pay the premium, and the important decision is, who do you want to be the beneficiary? It can go into a trust, to a company, or to one or more heirs. You want to talk to the people involved and possibly an estate attorney to figure out what the best plan is for you.

But don't let it stop you from getting the policy now. You can usually change beneficiaries later. Get that insurance. That way you know if something goes terribly wrong, at least this part won't make things worse. I have a friend who discovered when she was widowed that her husband had taken out a life insurance policy with her as the beneficiary. She was so touched! It helped her in her grief to know that her husband had loved her enough to make sure she would be financially safe. That's the beauty of life insurance—it's a final gift that lets your loved ones know how much you cared.

One other quick thing on this subject: Some people worry about insurance companies or insurance salespeople making money off of them. They resent the company's profit or the salesperson's commission. I don't worry about that at all. Everyone has to make a living. What they get actually has nothing to do with you. Your only focus should be on the value you get.

Other Insurance

Just as it's necessary to think about protecting your family if you were to die, it is also important to think about protecting yourself and your family if something crazy happens while you're still alive. Insurance exists to take care of an emergency such as fire or liability. Once, a parking garage at one of my properties caught fire. Luckily, no one was hurt, but there was a lot of property damage, not just to the structure, but also to the cars parked in it. But I had insurance. All I had to do was call up my agent and ask them to take care of it, and they did. That is peace of mind!

You don't just want to have insurance because their agents will take care of claims; you also want them for their lawyers. We live in a very litigious society. If you're on the hook for, say, a personal injury claim, you would have to hire your own lawyer. But in my opinion, the best lawyers in the business often work for insurance companies because they get the most experience sorting out all kinds of cases. I was sued by a guy who had double-parked and then, despite his mobility issues, cut across landscaping rather than walking on the path and, surprise, he fell and hurt himself. Those insurance lawyers were on it immediately, and even if they hadn't won, my insurance was in place to protect me from a potential $50,000 loss.

The amount you pay for insurance is worth every penny because you can sleep at night knowing that you're not vulnerable. The potential of earthquake or fire damage is not nearly as likely as the possibility of someone suing you. It can be really expensive to not have the right insurance; it could even wipe out your company. Liability insurance is an absolute must, and relatively speaking, it's a small part of your overall budget.

So we're agreed (I hope) that your home, your car, your business, your ability to work, and your life all need insurance. But buyer beware! Read all the fine print. There are predatory companies that make it so the cow has to jump over the moon before you can collect on your policy. Insurance is only worth getting (and it is worth getting!) if you can make a claim when you need it. You want to make sure you can understand exactly what's in the policy. Even the person selling the insurance may not know exactly what they're selling. So take time, do your research, and spend the money it takes to get the protection you need.

Captive Insurance

There is another option for insurance if you really want to protect your business. A "captive insurer" is generally defined as an insurance company that is wholly owned and controlled by the owners of the business it insures. It can insure the risks of its owners, and those it insures benefit from the captive insurer's underwriting profits.

Captive insurance was not fully promoted in the past, but is gaining momentum because of its financial benefits. The federal government's income tax laws do provide for premium deduction for captive insurance companies. Some states, however, do not allow captive insurance companies, although it is easy to incorporate in the states that do allow for it, such as Maryland.

When you need insurance for anything from flooding to product liability to malpractice, but going to an insurance company for coverage results in an excessive premium, captive insurance is the alternative. You pay the premium to your own company, which is tax deductible just as if you were paying to an outside insurance company. You build up your reserves in anticipation of a loss. If the premium exceeds your losses, you get to keep your reserves and you may be able to invest those reserves. The cost of setting up captive insurance and following the regulations is negligible compared to the premium reserve you build up. Again, this is one of the things I'm happy to show you exists, but I'm not telling you to run out and do it today. Get professional advice about your particular situation, your state, and your options.

Annuity

Before leaving insurance, let me make mention of annuities. An annuity is not an investment tool. It's a hybrid, something in between insurance and having your own stock portfolio. Unlike life insurance, the payout money is for you or whoever you designate. Generally, fees and commissions are high for this type of investment and the final return on it is much less than you would get from a comparable investment in mutual funds or exchange funds. So why do it? Because it has certainty.

The concept behind an annuity is to keep you from worrying about outliving your money, and that can provide tremendous peace of mind. There are many types of annuities. Typically, they are sold by insurance companies and provide steady payments for either a set period of time or for the rest of your lifetime. The simplest contract provides for a single lump-sum premium and/or regular payments, which will then be invested for you so the money will be there for you later in life, on a regular schedule. As with life insurance, premiums depend on the investment amount, your age, and the age you'll be when the payouts start. Many annuity features are available to customize for your needs.

Both you and the holding company take little or no risk because at first, all you do is pay into the fund. The financial institution handling the annuity invests your money with an eye toward paying it back to you later on a predetermined schedule. The company works the probability of the payments in their favor to cover their overhead and profit, while you have the peace of mind that you're putting money aside that will be there for you on a regular basis later in life.

My dad bought a $10,000 annuity each for my brother and me when I was eight years old. Dad purchased the annuities during the Depression; he wanted to be sure we had something to start our lives with when we were adults. It was his way of showing responsibility and love, and it helped me start my own business. That kind of foresight is something all parents should consider.

Taxes

Taxes are the source of government funding. All government activity uses tax collection as a form of income. Taxes fund our military and protect our borders. When there's a pandemic, these funds give the government leeway to help. Taxes also pay for the interest and repayment on bonds and projects to take care of roads, bridges, schools, and infrastructure. But taxes aren't cheap. About 30 to 40 percent of all income goes to some form of tax, including federal and state income taxes, property tax, luxury tax, "sin" tax (on things like cigarettes and alcohol), and sales tax. Income taxes on are on a progressive system. The more your income, the greater the percentage you pay in taxes. Tax Freedom Day is a significant date because it represents how long Americans as a whole have to work in order to pay the nation's tax burden. For instance, the pay you earn for the first seventy-six working days each year only just covers your tax payment. Tax Freedom Day in 2019 was April 16, the first day in which the money you earned didn't go to pay taxes.

The tax code is complicated because it attempts to serve a huge number of situations. Governments also provide tax incentives for social direction; in the simplest form, a "sin" tax on cigarettes is meant to decrease the amount people smoke and improve their (and our nation's) health. For business considerations, allowances are given for investments: machinery, real estate, research, and mineral explorations. For personal considerations, donations to charity, high medical expenses, and local taxes may also reduce the amount you pay in income taxes.

One thing about charity donations: Some people grump that you're only making a donation because of the write-off, that it somehow taints your intentions. I don't have to tell you what I think of that! Your donations should follow your values, of course, and if the government wants to reward people for helping others, that's great. But a tax write-off doesn't replace the money you paid. You wouldn't make a donation if you didn't have a good heart. Choose organizations that are doing good work in the world and give whatever your heart tells you. Ignore the naysayers.

You have legitimate, legal choices to reduce your tax. Putting some money into an IRA can, for many people, reduce their taxes and help set up financial stability for their retirement; that's a win-win. To maximize your ability to create wealth, you should look for opportunities to build wealth that, at the same time, limit what you have to pay. Obviously, this is something that requires research and, whenever possible, expert advice. This is well beyond the scope of this book, and I don't mean to tell you what to do, only to let you know that options do exist.

Funding your IRA is one obvious choice, but corporations are another. Corporations are taxed at a lower rate than individuals. Perhaps you'll want to think about setting up a corporation. A lot of people hear me suggest this and think it's only for the rich. That's not true. You can set up a corporation for a few hundred dollars. It also can factor into your liability—with everything you do, there's some possibility of being sued. Consult a professional on this and all tax matters for ways to limit both your tax and your liability exposure; it's well beyond the scope of this book, but I want you to know that options exist.

Pensions set up within a corporation can provide tax benefits, as during the period of time the pension is earning money, it is tax-free. As with a traditional IRA, the taxes are only paid at retirement, with the probability that your income will be less at that point and your tax bracket lower.

Partners can also divide their income by creating partnerships, which, again, might help you stay at a lower tax rate. And you can see what expenses might be able to become business expenses, again lessening your amount of taxable income.

Finally, trusts can be set up or gifts can be given to your beneficiaries while you're still around to watch them enjoy it. You always want to conduct your business legitimately, and that includes paying your taxes, but you also want to take advantage of the opportunities the tax code provides.

Different states have different tax laws, so you might want to invest outside of the state you live in. For instance, if you buy land in a state that has advantageous property taxes and land sale regulations, that land can grow in value, and when you sell it, you won't be hit with a large tax burden. Or you can be a person who collects valuables. These are investments that defer profit because the growth is inherent; it doesn't appear until you sell it. Antiques, coins, stamps, and art are all things that appreciate intrinsically. The cost may seem high at the moment you purchase it, but rare things remain rare. If there's a limited supply, the value will go up and your wealth will build. You can even buy valuables in the name of your beneficiary, so you've essentially already passed that wealth on without worrying about estate taxes. I have a friend who bought forestry, a young planting of trees in Arkansas, in the name of his grandkids. The trees grew as the kids did, and they were able to sell them to pay for their college educations. That's foresight.

Obviously, be smart about your purchases. You probably won't be able to retire on your hoard of Happy Meal toys from the 1980s. Don't buy land in the desert that's fifty miles from a sewer line. Land in devalued or outlying sections of a city, on the other hand, are poised for growth ten, twenty, thirty years down the line because cities will eventually need to expand and those areas will be revitalized.

These kinds of investments are about the future. I don't like the term "loophole" because it seems like you're trying to get away with something. You're not. I like to think of it as "futuristic investments" because what you're doing is using the one thing at your disposal when you're young: time. Things become more precious: Land appreciates, vintage items become antiques. You have to have the mind-set that everything, from the home you own to the art you buy, is part of your portfolio. People think only rich people can invest in things, but that's not true. Anything you're passionate and willing to learn about, even become an expert in, can be a path to investment. Local artists, Native American crafts, stamps, dollhouses, books . . . whatever hobby you truly enjoy could be a pathway to intrinsic, future investment. Remember my friend who essentially planted trees to send his grandkids to college? What he had was creativity, an agile mind, a willingness to look beyond the obvious and research the heck out of his options. You can do that, too. Be smart, be creative, be bold. Make the investment.

Finally, keep learning. This is not meant to be more than a quick primer on how to think about your taxes; you should always seek professional advice. But beyond that, you should keep learning. It's an absolute joy for me to go to a lecture or read a magazine article or learn about a new option or approach to personal finances, taxes, the stock market, everything. Don't put yourself at a disadvantage by thinking you know it all.

Chapter Thirteen

Your Legacy

As the years go by, you should be careful to not fall into a rut. If we let the tide pull us and just drift aimlessly, we don't use our potential. Real wealth is living a life of purpose. We were born to be creative, whether that means we pick up a paintbrush or discover a new way to run our business. When we take opportunities, we enrich our life. We don't always succeed, but the only real loss is in giving up. Self-fulfillment is the satisfaction of participating in the possibilities that are open to us.

Look for challenges and explore your surroundings. Having a middle-age crisis is not unusual; you may have accomplished so much that there doesn't seem to be anything else to look forward to. It's easy to give up and just relax, but the result is to fall into a nothingness. Instead, use the time to really enjoy and leverage what you have already built.

Retirement

We have an expectation that we are entitled to retire. Culturally, it's all set up for us at what age we can expect to leave our work. Many people look forward to that day, but for many others, boredom and uselessness set in after a lifetime of enjoying their work. Body and mind can break down; I used to see it a lot in men who didn't know what to do with themselves after spending a lifetime with the same company. Their routine had become all they knew how to do. This doesn't have to happen.

Health and well-being give us a lot more years to feel good, to be in our prime. Even if we don't want to keep working full-time, it doesn't have to be all-or-nothing. We can work part-time or fewer hours, or be of real service in a volunteer capacity. There is so much to accomplish when we refire our expectations of what we can do. Our years of experience, our wisdom, and our connections can still be of value. To be continually useful and productive is rewarding to both society and self-esteem.

Refiring, Not Retiring

It could be that you are able to retire when you're in your fifties—a good ten or fifteen years before most people retire. Maybe you've built a business that you have the opportunity to sell. Or you've paid off your loan debt, have built up your savings investment accounts, and your children have used the college fund you saved up to get their degree and strike out on their own. You might even want to consider moving to a less expensive state to live in. No matter what choices you have in front of you, instead of closing a door, think of it as opening one on a second life. This is your opportunity to do the kind of work or start the kind of business you've dreamed about. Redesigning your life, refiring on all cylinders, instead of retiring and turning into a couch potato, will add years, income, and health to your life.

Foundations

Retirement is also an opportunity to take on greater leadership in philanthropy. You can find a foundation that is doing work you admire; there are many that would welcome your active participation. There are thousands of foundations, including universities, libraries, research centers, animal welfare groups, educational associations, service organizations, hospitals—in every area of life, there is someone doing something to help. You can also set up your own foundation. It is not difficult to do, and the cost to get one started is negligible.

- Decide on a mission.
- Form a legal entity.
- File for tax exemption.
- Form a member board.
- Schedule meetings and create an accounting structure.
- Prepare a budget and open a bank account.

If you have run a business, you can definitely handle the creation of a foundation. This can be a marvelous way to create a second act for yourself, meet new people who share your values and interest, and really make a difference in the world.

Wealth Management

While you may have spent the earlier years of your life focused on accumulating wealth, now's the time to start thinking of how you want to disperse it. Money flows; it flows in and then it flows back out by taxation (to the government), by inheritance (to your loved ones), or through foundations (to charities and the greater community). Now is the time to start deciding how and where you want your money to flow.

Remember that wealth and money are not the same. Money can give you a safety net, but real wealth is in the knowledge that you will always be able to land on your feet. Having the ability to take care of your family and the freedom to make choices that allow you to be creative and involved in projects that stimulate you—that is wealth.

Sometimes, when you give money to your children, things don't work out as you planned. They're not miniature versions of you because they didn't lead your life. How many times have we heard of an individual who strove and faced adversity, starting out with little or nothing and sacrificing—trying, failing, and trying again—to relentlessly pursue their dream? And then, once they've achieved all of that, having the next generation take over with a completely different attitude? Their children didn't create the wealth; they are merely the caretakers of their inheritance. They are complacent—they don't actually know how to create wealth in their own right. By the third generation, they may be totally indifferent to the business they inherited and may be wasteful. A combination of mismanagement, estate taxes, and needless expenses chip away from the wealth their grandparents had established.

This isn't to make you unhappy, only to remind you that your children may not share your passion for your business. Talk to them about their own dreams and what they would want to relentlessly pursue. Don't just assume that their dream, or even their skill set, is the same as yours was. You'll only be setting yourself up for disappointment.

Today, more wealth passes from generation to generation than ever before, which means there are more estate counselors. Even insurance companies and stockbrokers have gotten in on the act and developed estate planning to help you figure out what to do with what you have. This has obvious value. If you're at that stage, definitely seek professional advice. As for me, I prefer to spend my time telling people how they can build something to begin with.

Finally, thinking about your legacy is more than just deciding what to do with the money you'll leave behind. How do you want to be remembered? What achievements do you want to serve as your legacy?

What is your mission in life?

Mission

There is a wise statement by a Chinese philosopher, Guan Zhong:

If you plan for one year, plant rice.
If you plan for ten years, plant a tree.
If you plan for one hundred years, educate others.

You can do all of these things. You can work on something that will bring you immediate income and the ability to meet your obligations (your rice), but you can also start work on something that won't come to fruition for years, whether it's a new invention, a novel, or property that will only appreciate over time (your tree). But you should also have that long-term plan, your hundred-year plan, to make sure that everything you do lines up behind a greater purpose.

I hope you have learned something in this book to help you as you search for your mission and fulfill your potential in life. May you succeed in all you do!

About the Author

Robert Barbera is a proud Italian American. His immigrant parents taught him the value of hard work and the importance of family. He made his first stock investment in 1954, only four years out of high school, and bought his first building in 1961. Through hard work, dedication, focus, and the support of his family, he now has 500 units and multiple subsidiary companies, making real estate the cornerstone of his success.

Throughout his life, Robert has built wealth not just for himself and his family, but also for many other people in fields as diverse as restaurants, car dealerships, and the financial industry. He launched The Barbera Foundation in 1994 and has donated his time, expertise, and financial resources to many worthy organizations, including Pepperdine University, Thomas Aquinas College, and the California State University system.

Robert was lucky in love, having had a happy, forty-five-year marriage to his late wife, Bernice, and finding love a second time around with Josephine, whom he married in 2003. He is the father of three wonderful children, Ann, John, and Patricia, and the grandfather of seven.

The Mentoris Project represents a piece of Robert's legacy. It connects his past, his parents, his children, and the future by honoring the achievements of Italians and Italian Americans and publishing inspirational books. Learn more at: www.mentorisproject.org

ACKNOWLEDGMENTS

Almost all the thoughts expressed in this book have to be credited to my parents and my brother. They each influenced the way I made choices: Dad in the simple love of peace and harmony, Mom in the optimistic fortitude to see life as a bowl of cherries, and Henry, who taught me that education is power.

I also want to acknowledge my late wife, Bernice, with whom I had forty-five wonderful years. She gave me undying support and patience during the tough times and kept us both headed in the right direction for a good life. Many thanks to my granddaughter Natalie, who has been my greatest supporter.

To the countless people who gave me a break, pointing me toward new opportunities, I also owe my thanks. I have been blessed with a wonderful second marriage, and so I thank my wife, Jo, for her support and for making allowances.

In my attempt to pass on to you all the information in this book, my deep appreciation goes to Laura Brennan for helping me find the right words.

Finally, thank you, reader, as well, for picking up this book and for taking charge of your own fortunes. I wish you well.

Now Available from the Mentoris Project

America's Forgotten Founding Father
A Novel Based on the Life of Filippo Mazzei
by Rosanne Welch, PhD

A. P. Giannini—The People's Banker
by Francesca Valente

The Architect Who Changed Our World
A Novel Based on the Life of Andrea Palladio
by Pamela Winfrey

A Boxing Trainer's Journey
A Novel Based on the Life of Angelo Dundee
by Jonathan Brown

Breaking Barriers
A Novel Based on the Life of Laura Bassi
by Jule Selbo

Building Heaven's Ceiling
A Novel Based on the Life of Filippo Brunelleschi
by Joe Cline

Building Wealth
From Shoeshine Boy to Real Estate Magnate
by Robert Barbera

Christopher Columbus: His Life and Discoveries
by Mario Di Giovanni

Dark Labyrinth
A Novel Based on the Life of Galileo Galilei
by Peter David Myers

Defying Danger
A Novel Based on the Life of Father Matteo Ricci
by Nicole Gregory

The Divine Proportions of Luca Pacioli
A Novel Based on the Life of Luca Pacioli
by W.A.W. Parker

Dreams of Discovery
A Novel Based on the Life of the Explorer John Cabot
by Jule Selbo

The Faithful
A Novel Based on the Life of Giuseppe Verdi
by Collin Mitchell

Fermi's Gifts
A Novel Based on the Life of Enrico Fermi
by Kate Fuglei

First Among Equals
A Novel Based on the Life of Cosimo de' Medici
by Francesco Massaccesi

God's Messenger
A Novel Based on the Life of Mother Frances X. Cabrini
by Nicole Gregory

Grace Notes
A Novel Based on the Life of Henry Mancini
by Stacia Raymond

Harvesting the American Dream
A Novel Based on the Life of Ernest Gallo
by Karen Richardson

Humble Servant of Truth
A Novel Based on the Life of Thomas Aquinas
by Margaret O'Reilly

Leonardo's Secret
A Novel Based on the Life of Leonardo da Vinci
by Peter David Myers

Little by Little We Won
A Novel Based on the Life of Angela Bambace
by Peg A. Lamphier, PhD

The Making of a Prince
A Novel Based on the Life of Niccolò Machiavelli
by Maurizio Marmorstein

A Man of Action Saving Liberty
A Novel Based on the Life of Giuseppe Garibaldi
by Rosanne Welch, PhD

Marconi and His Muses
A Novel Based on the Life of Guglielmo Marconi
by Pamela Winfrey

No Person Above the Law
A Novel Based on the Life of Judge John J. Sirica
by Cynthia Cooper

Relentless Visionary: Alessandro Volta
by Michael Berick

Ride Into the Sun
A Novel Based on the Life of Scipio Africanus
by Patric Verrone

Saving the Republic
A Novel Based on the Life of Marcus Cicero
by Eric D. Martin

Soldier, Diplomat, Archaeologist
A Novel Based on the Bold Life of Louis Palma di Cesnola
by Peg A. Lamphier, PhD

The Soul of a Child
A Novel Based on the Life of Maria Montessori
by Kate Fuglei

What a Woman Can Do
A Novel Based on the Life of Artemisia Gentileschi
by Peg A. Lamphier, PhD

Future Titles from the Mentoris Project

A Biography about Rita Levi-Montalcini
and
Novels Based on the Lives of:
Amerigo Vespucci
Andrea Doria
Antonin Scalia
Antonio Meucci
Buzzie Bavasi
Cesare Beccaria
Father Eusebio Francisco Kino
Federico Fellini
Frank Capra
Guido d'Arezzo
Harry Warren
Leonardo Fibonacci
Maria Gaetana Agnesi
Mario Andretti
Peter Rodino
Pietro Belluschi
Saint Augustine of Hippo
Saint Francis of Assisi
Vince Lombardi

For more information on these titles and the Mentoris Project, please visit
www.mentorisproject.org

Made in the USA
Middletown, DE
05 February 2025

70231400R00102